The Fair Par Guide To

RHODE ISLAND GOLF

Find Your Favorite Courses
Play Better Golf
Have More Fun Doing It

By

Stephen Heffner

Bogey Press – 2000

"The hole is small,
And really far.
I need more strokes
In my par."

- Dr. Henry Valentine
  (20–handicapper)

Dedication

Rhode Island might be the smallest state in the nation, but it is blessed with an abundance of wonderful golf courses. This book is dedicated to the golfers who populate these courses, and particularly to the under-appreciated folk among them known as recreational golfers – a group also described as duffers, hackers, choppers, and worse, by the less charitable among us.

They are not the sort of golfers one sees on Saturday and Sunday afternoons on television, swinging like poets and stroking putts like bankers making large deposits. They are, instead, the ordinary men and women of the golf world, who, for better or worse, have taken up the challenge of trying to find recreation in a game that is among the most difficult ever invented – a game whose numerous congenital cruelties routinely bring even the most optimistic players to their knees.

Although it might seem an endeavor of folly, they persevere. Day after day, week after week, sometimes in weather that would turn a mailman back, recreational players by the thousands troop to their local links and tee it up one more time. And while they might be short on skills, they are long on hope, models of bravery and persistence, heroes of the human spirit, fighting death and bogeys so long as there is breath in their bodies and available starting times.

On a more practical level, they are also the foundation of the golf industry. Without them, Tiger Woods, David Duval, and the rest would be playing for applause and trophies only, instead of the ample cash rewards that recreational players, as the game's paying fan base, make possible.

In honor of these common foot-soldiers of golf, I offer this humble volume, in the hope that it not only will lead them to enjoyable places to play in Rhode Island, but that it will help them find true recreation once they get there.

Table of Contents

The Fair Par System

The Golf Courses

Fair Par Scorecards

Rhode Island Public Courses
Rhode Island Private Courses

The Fair Par System

Introduction

For all the sublime and even mystical attributes that have been attached to golf, the game is, in the end, an exercise in cold numbers.

Every hole has a number, a handicap rating, and a yardage measurement. Nearly all the clubs in a player's bag are numbered, and each club can be expected to propel the ball a predictable distance. And there is nothing subjective about being successful at golf. Rather, success is a number – the lowest number of strokes played, or the most holes won, in a given match or tournament.

Golfers mostly benefit from all this numerical orderliness, but there is one number that is the bane of recreational players, whether they realize it or not. That number is Par. Specifically Scratch Par, the official number of strokes players are expected to take on a given hole, and for 18 holes in total.

It is worth noting that things weren't always this way. When golf began, and for many decades afterward, there was no such thing as Par. You simply knocked the ball around the sheep pasture, took in some fresh air and exercise, and then you went home. You didn't finish under Par or over Par, you simply finished. If you played a match, you either won or lost, and there was no other opponent beyond your human ones – no unforgiving, absolute, numeric taskmaster lurking on the scorecard to judge whether you had succeeded or failed.

By the late 1800s, however, golfers had begun to accept the concept of a "ground score" – Par – a standard against which a person might measure his golfing progress. And that's when the trouble began for golfers who wanted to play the game merely for occasional recreation.

Mind you, the idea has merit, because it gives players something to shoot for, a fixed goal that they can pursue and that, if they reach it, rewards them with a sense of accomplishment in what otherwise can be a very humbling game. The problem is this:

> **The standard has been set so high that the vast majority of golfers who have ever teed up a ball have never shot Scratch Par for 18 holes, and they never will.**

What kind of a standard is that? you might well ask. It's easier to get into Heaven, for God's sake!

The Fair Par system has two principal aims: first, to bring common sense to bear on what should be expected of recreational players; second, to give players learning the game a graduated set of standards that would let them progress at a sensible pace and avoid the bad habits that come with trying to shoot 72, when their skills make shooting, say, 102 far more likely.

It turns out that the Fair Par system offers two other very positive by-products: it can make the game more plain fun for recreational players, and it can speed up play on the golf course – something players of all abilities can appreciate.

As for traditionalists, they have nothing to fear from Fair Par, for it does nothing to alter the Rules of Golf, the handicap system, or the way matches or tournaments are played. And it leaves Scratch Par intact for those who think they can hack it.

But for golfers who prefer not to labor under the burden of trying to achieve a Par that is more suited to professionals, Fair Par does what its name suggests: it makes Par fair.

Thoughts From a Pro

"Just because I have a driver's license,
does that mean I should try the Daytona 500?"
Fred Bruno,
Head Professional, Rhode Island Country Club

The above question is posed by Mr. Bruno to make a point – not about auto racing, but about golf. Specifically, about the relationship between recreational golfers and Scratch Par.

Bruno has been the PGA club professional at Rhode Island Country Club for more than a quarter-century. In that time he has given literally thousands of lessons, and he has watched one recreational golfer after another struggle with unrealistic expectations – including trying to shoot Scratch Par.

Bruno's conclusion, based on all that observation, is this: "Scratch Par for recreational golfers just doesn't make sense."

The problem begins with the beginners, says the pro. "I've watched them beat themselves up trying to shoot Scratch Par, and they find the situation so demanding that it turns them off. I'd like to have a penny for all the golf clubs sitting in basements of people who got discouraged because they thought golf was too hard."

Once recreational players pass the beginner stage, says Bruno, their golf games improve, but rarely enough to match their lofty ambitions – which are fueled, in large part, by trying to achieve the impossible standard of Scratch Par. The result is that they play from the wrong tees, with the wrong clubs, and with the wrong strategies.

"Instead of playing from the white tees the way they should, they'll go to the blue tees, or the black tees, or the gold tees, or whatever the farthest tees are – and then the course annihilates them.

"Then, they'll play with clubs they can't handle. You'll see guys paying with a stiff-shafted Big Bertha driver with a 7.5 degree loft, and they're complaining because they can't hit the ball in the air.

"And, when they get in trouble, they'll try for miracle shots. They'll get in the woods, and they'll find an opening an inch and a quarter wide and try to hit the ball through it, even though the diameter of the *ball* is bigger than that."

The solution, says Bruno, is for recreational players work to improve their games and, at the same time, to recognize their limitations and play within them. One step in that direction is to play to a more lenient standard of Par, such as that set by Fair Par. "If golfers would accept it, they would enjoy themselves more. And they'd make more birdies and pars, instead of bogies and double-bogies."

He also advises the Fair Par system for beginners. "It's a realistic way to start to play. It will help you avoid putting so much pressure on yourself that you can't play at all. It's something that can teach you to play within yourself."

There's only one problem, says Bruno: the male ego. "There's no question it would help a lot of guys, if only they would accept it. The problem is we're dealing with egos. We're dealing with guys who've spent all kinds of money to buy the kind of clubs Brad Faxon and Billy Andrade have in their bags, and they take those clubs to the back tees and try to play like pros."

Bruno says those kinds of golfers could learn plenty from their wives and kids. "Women are much smarter than men. Women will recognize their limitations. Kids are the same way. If the men would do more of that, they'd be a lot better off. And they'd enjoy themselves more."

The last point, after all, is the most important thing Bruno thinks Fair Par has to offer. "It's a system that tries to make golf more fun for more people. And that's the way it should be."

The Fair Par Principles

Imagine, for a moment, that you've decided to join the high school track team and you want to become a high jumper.

You head out to the field after classes and find your coach waiting for you at the high jump pit. He explains proper high jumping technique. He goes through the motions of the approach, the spring, and the roll over the bar. He has you make a few practice jumps without the bar in place. Then, he says, "Ready to try a real jump?"

"Sure am," you say.

"Good," he says, and he proceeds to set the bar at the 7-foot mark, almost as high as the ceiling in your house. He claps his hands and shouts, "Have at it!"

Ridiculous? Of course. Nobody learns to high jump like that. The reality is that you start with the bar quite low. You master your technique as you work with a height you can manage. As your skills improve, you add power to your jumps, and you raise the bar little by little.

Then, one day, when you finally are ready, you set the bar at a championship height, and you go for it.

Now, let's do some more imagining. Let's imagine that you want to take up golf. You buy some clubs. You go to the practice range. Maybe you take some lessons from a professional instructor. Soon, you're ready to head for the course to play your very first round of golf.

You pay your greens fees and walk to the first tee. You came by yourself, so the starter places you with three other players, one of whom turns out to be the great Tiger Woods. As you stand next to Mr. Woods on the tee, he flips open his scorecard, and on it you notice that Par for him is listed as 72. Out of curiosity, you check your own scorecard, and, believe it or not, your Par is also listed as 72!

This can't be right, you think, and you rush back to the pro shop. Sure enough, all the scorecards are the same. Every player gets a card that pegs success at 72 strokes, and failure at anything worse. The game of golf has set the bar as high for you as it has for Tiger Woods. What's a duffer to do?

What indeed? Seems like you have only one choice: try to play

11

like a Tiger. Swing for the fences. Hit the driver on every tee. Never lay up. Aim straight for the pin on every approach. Never be content to just play it safe. Go for broke. How else can you shoot 72?

Okay, the foregoing contains a bit of fantasy, but not all that much. In truth, the only unlikely part is that you will ever meet Tiger Woods on the first tee. What is, unfortunately, quite real is the certainty that you routinely will be expected to play to a Par that is far more suited to Tiger's talents than to yours. And with the bar, in effect, set higher than your head, your natural reaction will be to try to clear it – which brings us to the first of the Fair Par Principles:

> **In trying to achieve impossible scores, such as Scratch Par, recreational golfers can end up playing worse, not better, than they should.**

The symptoms of trying to overachieve are many. Players swing too hard, and they end up whipping the golf club around in all directions, out of control. They jerk their heads up, desperate to follow the flight of the ball even before they have actually struck it. They rush the take-away, they rush the downswing, they jump at the ball, they lose their footing.

They also lose perspective, which renders them unable to tell the difference between a good strategy and a stupid one. They try to clear hazards when lay-ups are in order. They shoot for treacherously placed pins instead of the fat of the green. They try for miracle shots instead of safe plays out of deep rough, bad fairway lies, trees, bunkers, or other trouble spots.

It is a malady that fosters impatience and poorly controlled aggressiveness both in a player's swing and in his strategic approach to playing individual holes. But it is also an understandable problem, given, for example, that a recreational player can face a hole that plays 430-yards into the wind, and when he looks at his scorecard, he finds it saying to him, "Put the ball in the hole in four shots or you're a chump!"

Nowhere on his card, or anywhere else for that matter, does it say, "Hey, relax. Five would be a great score on this hole." Or, "Take it easy. Make six here and move on. There are easier holes coming." Because Fair Par sets a more lenient standard, it allows players to relax, play less desperately and more intelligently, and, as a result, score better than if they were trying to shoot Scratch Par. The second Fair Par principle, then, is a corollary of the first:

> **With Fair Par, a recreational golfer can raise the quality of his play by lowering his expectations.**

One of the worst things about forcing Scratch Par on all golfers indiscriminately is that it can induce in a beginner sufficient anxiety to ruin hours of good instruction and patient practice – and that raises the third of the Fair Par Principles:

> **Playing golf with a Scratch Par scorecard in your hand is the hard way to learn the game.**

Golf instructors might differ on the minor points of golfing technique, but virtually all strive for the same general thing for their students: to develop a smooth, unhurried, balanced swing.

The first step in building such a swing occurs on the practice range, where the instructor might not even ask the student to try to hitting a ball at first, but merely to swing the club until the player starts to get the hang of it. Even when the instructor lays out some balls for the student to hit, he doesn't care particularly where they go, or how far they go. What he cares about, still, is the swing, and whether the swing results in solid contact with the golf ball.

Only after a while does the instructor begin concerning himself with what direction the balls are going, or their trajectory. And only after that does he bother to pay attention to how far they travel.

A good instructor will try to instill that same sequence of priorities in his students, and that's easy to accomplish on the range. The challenge comes when the student walks from the practice tee to the first tee. Now, things are different. Now, the stakes are higher. There's a hole out there, it's a long way off, and it won't be easy to get to, what with all those bunkers, and that pond, and, yes, the wind.

Thank God, it's a Par-5, the student thinks. Then, he opens his scorecard and finds that he is facing a Par-4, more than 400 yards long. Now what? The peace and patience of the practice range seem a distant, vague memory. The blood pressure rises. The hands grow moist and tense as they grip the driver. The muscles in the shoulders tighten. And the first swing is…well, ugly, as are the results.

Why? Par is why, specifically Scratch Par, and the anxiety over trying to measure up, to attain the impossible, to avoid failure, which, as far as the student can tell from the scorecard, is anything worse than a four on that first hole, followed by similarly harsh demands on the succeeding 17 holes.

With a Fair Par scorecard in hand, however, the budding golfer not only can afford to relax a little more on that first hole, but for the entire round. Both his psychological and strategic approach to his round can now change, as he learns to manage each 18-hole journey as if he were managing a stock portfolio, weathering ups and downs with patience, and always keeping the overall bottom line in mind.

The fourth and last general principle of Fair Par is aimed at explaining how the more lenient and realistic system can help to lift the pall of failure from the shoulders of recreational golfers.

Indeed, one would be hard pressed to name another sport in which recreational participants are so reliably doomed to failure before they even begin to play as they are when they step into the world of Scratch Par. Sure, you might win a match against your buddies during a round, but unless you shoot 72 or so doing it, you will leave the golf course with only half a victory, for once again you will have been defeated by Scratch Par. Which brings us to this:

> **Golf has become a popular form of recreation in spite of, not because of, the pervasive sense of predestined failure that Scratch Par brings to the game. Golf stands only to benefit by making success more accessible.**

With that in mind, let's make sure we are not scaring anybody in the golfing establishment, and let us emphasize the following:

1. Fair Par is not meant to replace Scratch Par, only to serve as an alternative for players who prefer it.

2. Fair Par changes none of the other traditional parts of golf – not the Rules of Golf, nor the handicap system.

3. All Fair Par does is place a different scorecard into a player's hand, and a different point of view in his head.

The Fair Par System

It's a system that gives a player a scorecard that says he has accomplished something if he shoots 85, or even 95, for 18 holes. It tells him he doesn't have to hit every drive 300 yards, take risks from trouble spots, or aim approaches right at every deviously placed pin.

It's a system that allows the budding student golfer to walk from the practice range to the first tee, look at that 400-plus-yard opening hole, and not get nervous. Why? Because his scorecard says he has at least five shots to get there, maybe six. Then, instead of forgetting what he has learned in practice, he can stay calm, swing easily, keep his head down, and put the ball in the fairway.

And, it's a system that lets a player take close to 100 strokes on a particularly tough golf course and go home a success, having shot Par – a Par that was fair to his capabilities.

Clearly, none of that serves to harm the institution of golf in any way. On the contrary, it benefits golf in two important ways. First, it offers the recreational golfer greater hope for success at the outset, and, therefore, a better reason to want to play the game in the first place. Second, it offers the player a better chance of leaving the course happy, rather than discouraged, thereby increasing the chance that he will be eager to return.

The Fair Par Ratings

The Fair Par rating system reflects the game of golf itself, for it is a mix of science and art, demanding both cold logic and seat of the pants reckoning.

Like both the Slope rating system and the traditional USGA rating system, Fair Par considers all the elements that make a golf hole, and a golf course, difficult or easy, including yardage, bunkers, hazards, wind, narrowness of fairways, changes in elevation, size and challenges of the greens, and so on.

Unlike the two other rating systems, however, Fair Par does not have the luxury of making incremental ratings for each hole – the decimal fractions of the USGA ratings, or the expansive point system of Slope – and then merely adding up a total. In Fair Par, each hole must have a fixed, whole number as its Par, and then those numbers are added together to determine Par for the entire course.

One other important difference between Fair Par and the USGA's rating systems is the target audience. The USGA has always had its focus squarely on golfers who play at the top levels – professionals and committed amateurs, golfers who expect to make or break Scratch Par, either once in a while or routinely. As a result, for many, if not most, of the courses the USGA reviews, particularly the public courses, the association's Scratch Par rating is more demanding than that set by the course itself.

Fair Par, on the other hand, is concerned with two different levels of players: those whose expectation is to break 90, and those who tend to score in the vicinity of 100 or more for 18 holes. The members of the former group are classified as Level 1 players and the latter Level 2.

Rating Criteria for Level 1

The first, and probably most important, parameter that Fair Par considers is yardage.

Nearly all holes under 180 yards in length are likely to be rated as Par-3s at Level 1. Fair Par recognizes, however, that the closer the distance gets to 200 yards, the more tempted players are to pull woods, instead of irons, from their bags, and woods are notorious for having minds of their own, especially in the hands of recreational players.

If the hole is wide open and relatively trouble free, smacking a wood off the tee might be the right thing to do. But, if there is significant trouble to one side of the green or the other, or if being over the green is a worse scenario than being short, then Level 1 is more likely to set Par for the hole at four.

Why? To encourage players to leave the wood in the bag, and, instead, to play an iron shot, with the front edge of the green in mind. If the player strikes the iron well, odds are he'll be on the green. If he hits it less than perfectly, he'll be short of the green – but he'll also be short of the trouble areas, and in good shape to pitch onto the green and still have a chance at making a three.

In other words, by hitting the iron off the tee, the player stands a good chance of making four or better. If he hits a wood from the tee, he could well end up in a spot from which making five or six would be more likely.

On the majority of holes under 350 yards long, Level 1 Par remains at four, but as the yardage approaches the upper 300s, Fair Par starts to move toward making the holes Par-5s. The consideration concerns the sorts of clubs a player might be tempted to hit on the second shot, and how hard he might be tempted to try hit them.

It is not unreasonable, for example, to ask a Level 1 player to hit a tee shot 200 yards and keep the ball in the fairway, providing that the landing area is wide enough and relatively straight off the tee. On a 350 yard hole, that would leave the player an approach of only 150 yards, a distance that he should be expected to negotiate without incident, no matter what difficulties lie between him and the green.

But, using the reasoning we've discussed regarding Par-3 holes, to ask the player to hit a second shot that begins to approach 200 yards becomes complicated. First, he must play it from whatever lie his tee shot has left him. He also must play it from whatever angle he has left himself. And because of the increased distance to the green, any trouble that lies between him and the hole now looms larger. With only three more shots left to make Par-4, the player could grow nervous and be tempted to play a shot that is not in his best interest in the big picture.

If the hole is rated a Par-5, however, much of that anxiety will vanish, and the player can begin to think in terms of playing a smart shot, rather than a desperate one – which is exactly the sort of reasoning that Fair Par employs as the holes, and particularly the approach shots, increase in distance and difficulty.

As holes approach or exceed 400 yards, they become Level 1 Par-5s almost automatically. The point at which a hole becomes a Par-6, however, is often nearer to the cutoff for a Par-5, in terms of yardage, than a Par-5 is to a Par-4, or the Par-4 is to the Par-3. Why? Because the longer the hole, the more shots a player is required to hit, and the more shots he hits, the greater the likelihood is that he will hit a bad shot.

Even if a hole measures 250 yards, for example, we're only taking about one major stroke, the tee shot, and after that it's only a matter of pitching and putting. As a hole stretches toward 375 yards in length, we're talking about two strong strokes, and as we approach 450 yards and beyond, there might be three substantial, consistent strokes required, and that can be a lot to ask.

Certainly, by the time a hole measures 500 yards, Fair Par is disposed to giving Level 1 players the cushion of taking six strokes to make Par. (It would be a very rare instance, however, in which a Level 1 player is allowed seven shots to make Par.)

Based on that general criteria, you can see that it's possible to rough out a pretty accurate first draft of a Fair Par scorecard for a given golf course based largely on the length of individual holes.

The next step is to refine that rough draft by determining whether the layout of the holes, and the complications of bunkers, hazards, trees, terrain, wind, and the rest will make the holes play longer than the posted yardage, or whether the relative absence of difficulties, or a downhill slope or a following wind, make the holes play shorter. Of course, the hazards and other difficulties themselves might warrant adding strokes, regardless of whether they add yardage.

As we noted earlier, Fair Par ratings for individual holes need to be made in whole numbers, and that raises the issue of what to do in cases where several similar holes tend to fall in between one Par and another – say, between four and five. To leave them all at Par-4 would be too severe, but to make them all Par-5s would be too lenient. So, it can become necessary to split the difference and rate some as Par-4s and the others as Par-5s.

Or, let's say a golf course has four difficult, but not long holes that are rated individually as Par-3s, but that cumulatively are worth more than 12 strokes. None of the holes might be longer than 180 yards, so it might not be appropriate to rate any of them at Par-4. The next best thing is to have another look at holes that have been rated at Par-4 and Par-5 to see if there might be another stroke or two allowance to found there.

Another bit of subjectivity that can balance the whole is sometimes available on the opening hole of a course. There, the argument can be made that even a relatively easy hole can play tough, because recreational golfers rarely step onto that first tee properly warmed up.

Fair Par, then, is a system in which individual holes can have the same Par, yet not be exactly as easy or difficult as one another – but, if the rating has been done carefully, the total Par for 18 holes will be an equitable one.

Rating Criteria for Level 2

Compared with the process of establishing a Level 1 rating, determining the Level 2 Fair Par is relatively simple.

To begin with, every hole at Level 2, with few exceptions, is rated automatically at a minimum of one stroke above Scratch Par. (Exceptions might include holes measuring under 100 yards that feature virtually no trouble, or the occasional Scratch Par-4 or Par-5 hole that, for reasons unknown, simply has been overrated by the club's golf committee or by the course operators. These are rare and they also are obvious.) The result is that virtually all Level 2 Par ratings are a minimum of 18 strokes above Scratch Par on an 18-hole course.

After that, another stroke can be added to selected holes, and this is typically done when substantial distance, combined with trouble, is evident. Most holes exceeding 400 yards, for example, should qualify as Par-6s at Level 2, and most holes measuring 500 yards or more automatically earn a Par-7 rating. But shorter holes also can qualify for the double stroke allowance in cases where the amount of trouble the hole presents would require a Level 2 golfer to play with extra caution, or where, say, a particularly large water hazard is likely to swallow at least one shot from a Level 2 player.

One rule of thumb in establishing Level 2 ratings is that, if a hole seems to fall between a single or double stroke allowance over Scratch, the rating should err on the side of leniency. It is the Level 2 player, after all, who is likely to need forbearance the most, as the range of abilities in this group is broad, spanning golfers on the verge of breaking 100, to players with 120 or worse in their immediate futures.

The Level 1 player, by contrast, chooses that standard because he is convinced he can break 90 and wants a greater challenge. Leniency at Level 1, therefore, needs to be handed out more judiciously.

A Note on Tee Markers

In most cases, Fair Par ratings are made from tee markers that lie between the forward-most tees (or, in politically incorrect but traditional terms, the "ladies tees") and the back tees.

On many golf courses, these are still the traditional white tees, lying between the red tees and the blues, and the Fair Par ratings are taken from there for two reasons. First, the yardage from those tees is usually adequate to provide players at both Level 1 and Level 2 plenty of challenge. Second, it allows a progressive step for players who use Fair Par as a gradual process of improvement – that is, when a player can shoot Par at Level 1 or 2 from the white tees, he can then move back to the blue tees and try his luck from there.

On other courses, both new and old, the trend in recent years has been to install four sets of tee markers in a variety of colors. At some courses, this is done to establish a championship yardage from the deepest tees that is substantially greater than the yardage from the second deepest set. In those cases, Fair Par assumes that the very back tees are not a realistic option for recreational players, and therefore makes ratings from the middle set of the three remaining pairs of markers.

In some cases, however, the extra set of markers represents a more forgiving version of the traditional white tees, and, depending on the yardage from those tees and the overall difficulty of the golf course, the Fair Par rating can be taken from there.

No matter where the Fair Par ratings are made from, however, players at either Level 1 or Level 2 should feel free to play from any tee at which they are comfortable, including the most forward tees. Remember, golf is supposed to be recreation, not a frustrating exercise in trying to do the impossible. Try a shorter tee, and you just might like it.

Using Fair Par

If your goal is to use Fair Par merely as a way to relax and have a little more fun on the golf course, then all you need to do is grab a Level 1 or Level 2 scorecard, head to the links, and start knocking the ball around.

But if you want to use Fair Par as a tool to gradually improve your game, you will need to focus on two main ideas:

> **First, put Scratch Par out of your mind and sell yourself on the concept of Fair Par. Second, learn to use the allowances provided by Fair Par to manage your entire 18-hole game.**

The first step can be the most difficult, particularly if your personality leans toward the compulsiveness of a Type A ("I know I can shoot Scratch if I only try hard enough!"), or if you've got a little too much macho in you ("I'm gonna bring Scratch Par to its knees, damn it!"), or, perhaps, if you're the sort who would feel guilty about doing something as untraditional as using a scorecard other than the Scratch Par card ("What if somebody sees me?").

No matter what the psychological impediment, Fair Par will not work for you until you forget about Scratch Par and accept Fair Par as your primary objective. The Fair Par scorecard is designed to assist in that, for nowhere on the Level 1 or Level 2 card for a given golf course is there any mention of the Scratch Par, either for individual holes or for the golf course in total.

The trick is to trust the card. If it tells you that a hole is a Par-6 or Par-7, then that's what it is. If it tells you that Par for the round is 83, or 92, then that's what it is, and that's what you should strive for.

Of course, there's no avoiding the traditional signs that typically are posted on tees to provide the yardage, the Scratch Par, and sometimes a diagram of each hole. And if there are other players in your group who are not playing to Fair Par, you are sure to overhear them discussing Scratch Par as they go. In those cases, pay as little attention as possible. It is only the devil of Scratch Par trying to tempt you into trouble. Resist, and focus on your Fair Par goals.

A word of caution to experienced golfers: be prepared to battle your own skepticism when you first take up Fair Par, particularly when you step up to a hole that the scorecard rates as Par-6 or Par-7. At those moments, you might be tempted to stand on pride or your manhood (or womanhood) or something else just as silly, and say, "Who needs all those strokes?" The answer is, you do, until you're able to shoot Fair Par for the entire 18 holes at your chosen Level.

And that brings us to the second important idea in using Fair Par – strategic course management, with the overall goal of reaching the Level 1 or Level 2 Fair Par standard for 18 holes. At the heart of this notion is the need to accept the following thought:

> **Until you're within 15 feet or so of the hole, and you have your putter in your hand, every stroke you take is not an end in itself, but a means of setting up the next shot.**

Too many recreational golfers think only in the short term. They don't think past the shot they are about to make. They stand over their golf ball, determined to knock it absolutely perfectly, as if that would absolve them of having to accomplish anything else on the hole – as if making that one perfect stroke will solve all their problems.

It's an attitude that is doomed to failure, mainly because recreational players rarely hit the ball exactly as they would like, and when their plans for precision fail, they often leave themselves in less than desirable predicaments. Under the guidance of Fair Par, the idea is to avoid placing excessive demands on any given shot, and instead to find comfort zones to aim for – areas of fairway or green that are not only reachable, but that also will provide a good platform for playing the subsequent shots.

To illustrate that idea, let's review individual facets of the game, beginning on the tee.

Driving

As anyone knows who has ever whacked the No. 1 wood a mile in the wrong direction, the driver can get you into more trouble in less time than all the other clubs in your bag combined. The driver is like a chain saw: if you use it skillfully, you can get a lot accomplished in a short time; but if you're sloppy with it, it can leave you limping.

As conservative as the Fair Par approach might sometimes seem, by no means does it advocate that you leave your driver in your bag. Nobody's asking you to quit playing with the big dog. In fact, learning to play intelligently with the driver is at the heart of learning to play Fair Par golf, because if you can achieve golfing discipline with the long stick in your hands, you can achieve it everywhere else in your game as well.

The most important step in achieving that discipline is to recognize the following:

> **It is far less important how far you drive the ball than how your drive positions you for your next shot.**

Hitting a tee shot 300 yards is pointless, after all, if the ball ends up out of bounds, in the woods, in deep rough, in a difficult bunker, or in some other position that dims your chances for a good second shot.

You are better off to hit a shorter drive and have the ball end up in a spot that gives you a good lie and good look at your next shot. And if the only sure way to hit such a drive is to do it with a club other than the driver, there is no shame in that, only strategy.

In fact, as you review Fair Par ratings for individual holes, you'll notice that it is not unusual for a relatively short Scratch Par-4 to be rated a Fair Par-5 if it is a difficult or treacherous driving hole. The allowance is made to encourage players to realize that is better to be short and safe off the tee, rather than long and in trouble.

Long Second Shots

We're talking here about second-shot situations in which you are too far from the green to be able to reach it in one swing. Of all the shots you will routinely face on a golf course, these should be the proverbial "no-brainers."

Look at it this way. It's going to take you two shots to get to the hole from where you lie, no matter what. If your lie is good, there's little trouble up ahead, and you're inclined to hit a fairway wood, feel free. But if your lie is at all questionable, and if you could reach trouble by spraying a wood, then what's the point of hitting a wood? How much do you stand to gain over hitting, say, a 3-iron? Is it worth it?

It's nice to have a chip or a short pitch to the green for your third shot, but is it that much worse to have a full pitching wedge, or even a 9-iron or 8-iron? Particularly if the risk of hitting a wood on your second shot might mean taking four shots in all to get from the tee to the putting surface, instead of three?

Approach Shots

The goal in hitting an approach shot, of course, is to knock the ball onto the green. That sounds simple enough, but what recreational golfers often fail to give enough thought to is exactly *where* on the green the ball ought to go.

The thing that can cloud a recreational player's judgment most in these situations is the pin itself, for it can have the same affect on a golfer's attention as a matador's cape does on the bull: see the pin, aim for the pin.

That's not a problem if the pin happens to be cut smack in the middle of a flat green, but most greens aren't flat, they have slope – sometimes a little, sometimes a lot. And it almost always pays to be putting uphill rather than down, which means players need to think ahead and plan on leaving their approach shots below the hole, rather than above it.

Second, it's part of the challenge of the game – as well as crucial to the proper maintenance of a green – for the hole to be moved to different parts of the green from one day to the next. As a result, the hole eventually ends up being cut near one edge of the green or another, and players need to decide if hitting for those positions is worth the risk of missing the green entirely.

Consider two rules of thumb here:

> **No matter where the pin is, aim for the center of the green, or, at least, for a spot between the center and the pin. If you can't decide which of two clubs to hit, choose the more lofted club.**

Regarding the second point, unless there is a bunker or some other problem at the front of the green, it's usually better to be short than long. Slopes on greens tend to run downward from back to front, which means the shorter approach usually leaves the uphill putt you would prefer. And many greens are built up at the back edge and fall off steeply there, which makes for a difficult chip shot if you've hit the ball over. Conversely, many greens tend to be level with the fairway at the front edge, which provides a much more inviting chip shot.

One last point on approach shots is also something that applies to other most other shots as well:

> **The closer you play to trouble, the more often you will be in it.**

Sometimes you have no choice: if there's a bunker or some other piece of trouble lying directly across your line of play to the green, then you must play over it. But often, the bunker will lie a little to one side and a piece of the green will be visible to the other side. In those cases, even when the pin is directly behind the bunker, you are well advised to move your target line toward the available piece of green. For recreational golfers, being anywhere on the green, is better than being in the bunker.

By the way, the strategy for approach shots applies also to any tee shot on which the green can be reached in a single stroke. We're talking here about Par-3 holes and very short Par-4s.

Trouble Shots

The oldest rule for trouble shots is also the best rule for those shots under Fair Par:

> **When you're in trouble, simply get out of trouble the easiest way available. Above all, that means avoid doing anything risky just to gain a few yards of forward progress.**

If you've played any amount of golf, you've been in the following spot. You've hit into the woods and you have an easy route back to the fairway, providing you are content to merely punch the ball out sideways. It won't get you any closer to the hole, and maybe you even have to hit a bit backward, but at least it's safe.

Then, you look again and find another opening that would allow you to hit the ball forward, rather than just sideways. It would allow you to gain some yardage, and it wouldn't seem like a totally wasted shot. The only problem is, the opening isn't as big as the sideways opening. Or, maybe your swing is impeded by a bush or a branch. So, it's more risky. But you just hate to settle for that sideways punch. You want to be bold, you want to make something happen, so you chose the riskier shot.

Riskier indeed. Too frequently, the shot doesn't go as planned and the ball never makes it out of the woods. In the worst case, you end up in a spot where you have no choice but to play out sideways. Now, instead of wasting just one shot, you've wasted two – or more.

With the extra strokes provided by Fair Par, you possess the luxury of being able to play that first, safe, sideways shot without fear of falling too far behind Par. So play it. And the same goes for shots from any other trouble spot, where the first order of business should be to get out of trouble.

Pitches and Chips

View these as you would an approach shot, with the idea that you probably are not going to knock the ball into the hole except by dumb luck. So, your next best strategy is to identify the area of the green you would most like to putt from, and try to hit the ball in that vicinity.

Just as with an approach shot, don't be tempted to get too cute with green-side bunkers, particularly when you have to hit over one and the pin is cut directly behind it. Too often, recreational players try to play that shot the way a pro would, landing the ball a hair past the bunker and letting it trickle to the hole.

It's a nice idea, of course, but the frequent result is that the player doesn't hit the ball hard enough and it drops into the bunker. Now, instead of standing on the green with a putter in your hand, you're gripping that ugly sand wedge, you've already wasted at least one shot, and you're less than sure where the next one will end up.

Better to have been on the green in the first place, even it meant facing a long putt.

Putting

If you have followed the guidelines of Fair Par, and if luck has been with you, by the time you reach the green, you have avoided putting yourself in the position of having to sink a long putt to save a good score on the hole. Instead, you have put yourself in a position where all you need are two putts for a good score.

If your ball lies more than 15 feet or so from the hole, view the initial putt the way you have viewed all your other shots on the hole so far – as a setup for your next shot. That means you shouldn't be aiming directly for the hole so much as for an area around the hole, and preferably below the hole if the green has any slope to it.

The longer the putt, the larger an area you should aim for – although logic tells you not to consider an area so large that it would make sinking the second putt a chore. One traditional putting tip holds that you should imagine you are putting for a manhole cover. If that works for you, fine, but any similar imaginary device probably will work as well.

Above all, remember this:

> **Unless you're convinced the putt is within your range to be made in a single stroke, plan on taking two putts.**

That might not be an easy concept to swallow, because the natural tendency is to try to sink everything, and many golfers will view anything less as tantamount to cowardice. But if your overall goal is to shoot Fair Par for the entire round, avoiding 3-putt greens is crucial. A consistent pattern of two putts per hole, with the occasional 1-putt green thrown in, will go a long way toward helping you reach that goal.

Graduation

Once a golf course has received a Fair Par rating, golfers have three playing options: Scratch Par, Fair Par Level 1, Fair Par Level 2.

Many recreational players will never have the ability or desire to try to compete with Scratch Par. Instead, with a Fair Par scorecard in hand they can happily strive for a different level of golfing success, one that is within their reach, and, at the same time, will send them home with a solid sense of accomplishment if they achieve it.

For players who simply won't settle for less, in the end, than shooting Scratch Par, let's offer a quick summary of how to use Fair Par to get there.

You can use Fair Par the way a student of the high jump would view his task. You start low, you refine your technique, and little by little, you aim a little higher.

For the high jumper, this means starting with the bar below his waist and gradually moving it up, a few inches at time, until it is above his head.

For the golfer, it means playing to the Fair Par Level 2 scorecard from the shorter tees. When you can achieve that, you move to the back tees. When you can shoot Par at Level 2 from the there, pick up the Level 1 scorecard and head again to the shorter tees.

When you are finally able to reach Level 1 Par from the back tees, it's time to graduate to the Scratch Par scorecard, and to do so while maintaining the patience, poise, and technique you have acquired on the way up.

And then, if you're lucky, one day you can go out and bring the golf course, and Scratch Par, to its knees.

RHODE ISLAND PUBLIC COURSES

Bristol Golf Club

95 Tupelo Street, Bristol – 253-9844 – 9 holes

Scratch Par for 18 holes – 64
Fair Par Level 1 – 68
Fair Par Level 2 – 82

Located in the heart of the town and popular for it's convenient location and low greens fees, the Bristol Golf Club was once an 18-hole layout that was condensed to nine holes to make room for the industrial park that now surrounds the place.

It was also where one of Rhode Island's best known tour professionals, Billy Andrade, played as a youngster, learning the game in his own backyard before venturing on to the more famous, far-flung golf tracks of the world.

In reducing the golf course to nine holes, a previous private owner (the town is the present owner) was able to leave some holes intact, but he was forced to shorten and reconfigure others sufficiently that they amount to almost completely new holes. The result was a course that now features five Scratch Par-3 holes, three short Scratch Par-4s, and one medium length Scratch-5 – adding up to a 9-hole Scratch Par of 32.

Bristol GC is, in effect, an executive course where players can get plenty of work on their short games, while also being able to pull the driver from the bag on occasion – and maybe do it all during a long lunch break.

It is also distinctive for a pair of holes, #2 and #7, on which lines of artificial trees – utility poles supporting overhead wires – run the length of the fairways and become obstacles.

In fact, on #7, the poles close in from left side so tightly that, if they had branches and leaves as they did when they were live trees, this might qualify as the narrowest fairway on the planet.

The best golf hole on the course might be #3. It measures 148 yards to an uphill shelf of a green, which is well guarded in the front by bunkers, and falls off steeply in the back. Out of bounds runs closely up the right side of the fairway and pinches in as it nears the green.

The most attractive approach on the course might be found on

#9, a short, sharp dogleg left, on which the second shot, usually in the 100-130 yard range, plays over a pond to a green that is tucked back into a circle of overhanging trees.

The preponderance of very short holes at Bristol means that Fair Par at Level 1 is very close to Scratch Par – 68 to 64. Aside from holes #7 and #8, there are no other holes where Level 1 players can expect, or should need, an extra shot.

For the same reasons, players at Level 2 can expect nothing more than a single shot above Scratch on each hole, which puts Level 2 Fair Par at 82.

If you've never been to the Bristol Golf Club, one unusual feature is worth noting: the 19th hole, called The Clubhouse, is, in reality, a neighborhood tavern, complete with pool tables, electronic bar games, a large dining area, and an outdoor sand volleyball court.

In fact, the place could pass as just another friendly neighborhood bar if it weren't for two things: the golf course across the street, and the putting green immediately outside the front door.

Country View Golf Club

Colwell Road, Harrisville – 568-7157 – 18 holes

Scratch Par – 70
Fair Par Level 1 – 78
Fair Par Level 2 – 91

This aptly named golf course is, indeed, well out in the country – so much so, in fact, that reaching it may offer as much of a test of map-reading skills as you're likely to encounter trying to get anywhere in this state.

Nevertheless, enough people make the effort to get their golf with a "country view" that the place is as busy as it wants to be in the summertime.

Much of the golf course, particularly on the back nine, has the look and feel of an orderly park, with graceful weeping willows and other mature trees tidily spaced amid acres of level fairway.

Many players will tell you that the best golf hole on the course is #3, 485 yards long from the white tees. It is a good driving hole, because even though the drive disappears over a hill, the landing area is wide. The problem is the second shot, which brings into play an overgrown stream that lies in the bottom of a wide depression short of the green.

Carrying the water and vegetation with the second shot is not impossible, provided you've hit a good-sized tee shot. Even if you haven't crushed a drive, you can be tempted to try the fly-over because of an inviting few dozen yards of relative safety that lie between the far side of the water and the green. Still, it's a risk.

But laying up is not always a picnic either, for the fairway dives toward the stream, and if you hit your lay-up a shade too far, particularly in the dry months of summer, it stands a good chance of scooting straight into the mess below, never to be seen again.

In determining Level 1 Fair Par for the course, the back nine presents a bit of a problem, because there are several holes which, played from the white tees, fall into an in-between area for Level 1 players.

The holes – numbers 12, 13, 17, and 18 – are all between 340 and 350 yards long and offer fairly wide, level driving areas and not a great deal of trouble around the greens. Typically, these are the types of holes on which Level 1 players should be expected to make four most of the time, although if the holes are even a little longer, with a tad more trouble either in the fairway or around the green, they can qualify for an extra stroke.

Keeping all four holes at Scratch would mean that Level 1 Fair Par on back side would come in at 36, just a shot over Scratch, and that, cumulatively speaking, would not give Level 1 players a fair break for the nine.

The solution is to award an extra shot at two of the four holes.

The first choice is #12, where the 90-degree dogleg right prevents a player from taking advantage of a long tee shot, as the corner of the dogleg stands less than 200 yards from the white tees. Hitting it much farther doesn't gain the player much, unless he can put a big fade on the ball. A long straight drive, in fact, can take you farther from the hole, rather than closer.

The second choice is #18, which bends left around a sweep of willows that can either snag a drive hit too close to the corner, or, for players trying to avoid that, can force the tee shot to sail wide to the right – resulting, again, in a lengthier approach than you'd like.

Coventry Pines

1065 Harkney Hill Road, Coventry – 397-9482 – 9 holes

Scratch Par for 18 holes – 71 men, 72 women
Fair Par Level 1 – 79
Fair Par Level 2 – 94

If certain Rhode Island politicians had had their way some years back, this unpretentious country track might be under water today, or least off-limits to the public as part of the now-defunct Big River Reservoir project.

For years, some state officials had proposed flooding hundreds of acres in the area and setting aside hundreds more as a watershed. The idea was to build a reservoir water sufficiently large that it would provide all the drinking water that the state's residents would ever need.

In the 1970's, long before the Big River project had received all the necessary federal environmental permits, the state went about condemning and buying land, houses, and businesses in the area – including Coventry Pines.

The state allowed the course to stay open while negotiations and planning for the reservoir project continued, but golfers played here under the cloud that every round might be their last at Coventry Pines. Then, in 1990, under mounting criticism of the project by environmentalists, the federal government turned it down. The state protested, but the project was dead. There would be no Big River Reservoir.

So, what about all the property the state had purchased? Many thought that the state could just give it all back, but things just weren't that easy. Legal entanglements, combined with the state's desire to continue to control the watershed area, meant that the government would continue to own the majority of the property it had acquired, while leasing some of it to private owners, which is the case with Coventry Pines.

As for the golf course itself, it is divided distinctly into the lowlands holes – the first four and #9, all relatively flat and straight –and the uplands holes –#5 through #8, which climb, dive and curve about the course's rugged, heavily wooded interior.

The local rules advise golfers to play white tee markers as the front nine and red markers as the back side, but the difference between the two is not significant – except at #4. There, the red tees can be dozens of yards behind the white markers, a difference that on the Scratch Par scorecard changes the hole from a 484-yard Par-5, to a Par-4 that can be in excess of 400 yards long.

Either way, the hole can be difficult, particularly because it can play into the wind in the summer, and it qualifies for extra strokes at both Fair Par Level 1 and Level 2.

The best hole on the course is probably #6. At 520 yards, it demands a blind tee shot over a hill and down a narrow chute cut through the woods. At the bottom of the hill, a stream and marshy area cuts across the fairway and often catches players' second shots. When you finally get to the green, you find it raised above the fairway and tucked behind a tree. Again, players at both Level 1 and Level 2 qualify for extra strokes on this hole.

Also distinctive in its own way is #8. It is 187 yards long, and although it plays from an elevated tee, the green below is tucked so tightly against the base of the hill that golfers don't get a good view of it from the tee. So, a hand-painted bulls-eye has been nailed to a tree behind the green to provide direction.

The course finishes in panoramic fashion, as players hit out of the woods from an elevated tee to the wide open lowlands below.

Cranston Country Club

69 Burlingame Road, Cranston – 826-1683 – 18 holes

Scratch Par – 71
Fair Par Level 1 – 81
Fair Par Level 2 – 94

This handsome, well-kept golf course isn't the sort of place that first comes to mind when somebody mentions the busy, sometimes cramped, city of Cranston and the nearby area. It is, after all, only a matter of minutes from the bustle and traffic of the major shopping malls in Warwick, and even a shorter distance from the crowded environs of downtown West Warwick.

Therefore, it is nothing but a pleasant surprise to find this oasis of manicured green space off Burlingame Road.

Among its amenities, Cranston offers a practice range, and players are advised to hit a bucket of balls as soon as they get there. Why? Because Cranston isn't one of those courses on which a golfer can expect a benign opening hole, such as the short and pretty Par-3 first hole at Foxwoods-Boulder Hills (123 yards), or the 300-yard Par-4 first at Meadow Brook.

Instead, Cranston challenges players right away with the second longest hole on the course, 529 yards from the white tees, the number-one rated handicap hole on the front nine.

Despite being 120 yards longer than any other hole on the front side, however, it does establish the pattern of what to expect on the front: mostly level, fairly wide open fairways, leading to greens that all seem to have bunkers left and right, spaced by run-up openings in front.

The front nine also includes the most photogenic hole on the course, the 5th. From the white tees, it measures 346 yards and it bends gracefully to the right between dense stands of trees. Lying to the front and right side of the green is a pond, banked on the green-side by a handsome stone retaining wall.

Although the hole isn't particularly long from the white tees, Fair Par Level 1 players will get an extra shot here, for two reasons. The first is to encourage them to simply keep the ball in the fairway and out of the trees; second, to encourage them to play their approach shots long enough and far enough left to take the pond out of play.

That strategy on the approach shot might mean an extra putt on the large green, particularly if the pin is cut behind the pond on the right side, but that's better than trying to get too ambitious and ending up in the water.

The opening hole notwithstanding, players can be forgiven for growing a little comfortable on the front side, but that quickly changes on the back, where the terrain and the holes get decidedly rougher.

It begins on #10, which doglegs left from a high tee into a valley, and then back uphill, steeply, to the green. The 11th is very similar, except in the valley this time a pond lurks on the left.

There's more water on the 13th, lying in front and to the left of the green, a spot that can lure a player, who might be unconsciously favoring that side to stay away from woods that pinch in from the right.

Players get a bit of breather at holes 14-16, but the fun resumes in a big way on #17, probably the toughest hole on the course. At 545 yards, it plays through an undulating, right-sloping fairway, over water that cuts across the fairway in an area where a second shot might land, and uphill to a shelf of a green cut into a steep hillside.

After that, the nine finishes as it started, playing from a high tee into a deep valley, and all the way back up to the green.

As you might expect, Fair Pair allows players more shots over Scratch on the back side than the front, 6 shots to 4 at Level 1, and 12 to 11 at Level 2.

East Greenwich Golf and Country Club

1646 Division Road, East Greenwich – 884-5656 – 9 holes

Scratch Par for 18 – 72
Fair Par Level 1 – 80
Fair Par Level 2 – 94

This modest nine-hole track, set in the wilds of East Greenwich (what's left of them, anyway), has long been a popular destination for recreational players – and those golfers got an even better reason to tour this course after major changes were made here in 1999.

The biggest changes occurred on the 6th hole and on what was previously the 2nd hole. Beginning with the latter (now listed as hole #5 in a re-routing of the layout), it had been a straight, short (310 yards), uninteresting Scratch Par-4 – possibly the least distinguished hole on the course. In its new life, it is now one of the best holes on the course, measuring 385 yards from the white tees, and playing to a new green over the pond that once fronted the 6th green. To make room for this expansion, an entirely new 6th hole was built. While still a Scratch Par-3, the new #6 is a little shorter and less interesting than its predecessor (there is no pond), but the positive changes to old #2 more than offset the loss of some character on the 6th.

Another big change occurred on #7, which had previously been a somewhat difficult, 408-yard Scratch Par-4 hole, laid out in a partial dogleg left. Now, new blue and white tees have been cut into the woods, and they serve to straighten and lengthen the layout to a 475-yard Scratch Par-5. The old tees remain, but now hold only the red tee markers. Players looking to improve their scores are happy with the change, given that the Scratch Par allowance has gone up one stroke, while the hole was lengthened by less than 70 yards – a trade-off that works in the recreational golfer's favor.

As for the re-routing, the sequence of four holes changed, as #2 became #5, #3 became #4, #4 became #2, and #5 became #3. (It is worth noting that this new mapping returns the new 2nd and 3rd holes to the positions they originally held when the course was built.)

The best hole on the course, #5, remained unchanged in the latest renovations. It is the longest hole on the track, playing 500 yards from an elevated tee set on a tall rock outcropping, down to a fairway that is lined tightly on the left by dense woods and on the right by more trees and a stream. Woods and a wetland appear farther up on the right, and, just short of the green, the stream cuts diagonally across the fairway.

While the view from the high tee is lovely, this is a case where the elevation is not necessarily an advantage. Why? Because it allows drives to carry farther than they otherwise would, and to reach more trouble in the process. The result is that it becomes very easy to knock the ball into or behind the trees on either side of the fairway. The problem is compounded by the sort of thoughts that can creep into a player's mind on this tee – thoughts like, "Man, I could really crank one from here and maybe get on the green in two." Of course, that's exactly the sort of thinking that leaves a golfer trying to get on the green in five or six after he has driven into big trouble.

The better strategy is to use the Fair Par allowances – the hole is a Par-6 at Level 1 and Par-7 at Level 2 – to take a deep breath and recognize that both the fairway and the approach to the green are so tightly guarded by trees and the stream that getting home in two shots is unlikely. So, the better play is to hit a safe, controlled tee shot, in the knowledge that such a drive, combined with a safe second shot, will leave you within a very short iron shot of the green, instead of in trouble.

One other hole on which players can use Fair Par allowances to be strategic and safe is the 387-yard 8th, where a substantial pond that fills the fairway can be reached from the tee. The hole is rated a Level 1 Par 5, and players should use the extra shot to be patient, making sure to hit the ball short enough to avoid flirting with the water. It might mean a slightly longer approach to the green than you'd like, but at least you'll be playing the shot from dry land.

Exeter Country Club

320 Victory Highway, Exeter – 295-8212 – 18 holes

Scratch Par – 72
Fair Par Level 1 – 82
Fair Par Level 2 – 94

This course has long been a favorite of residents of South County, and as highway access to rural Exeter has improved over the years, it has become a popular destination for golfers from all over the state. Why? Because it is a pretty place that offers pretty darn good golf.

On the first point, the course would make a lovely place just to walk, even if you weren't out there to play golf. It boasts such a wonderful variety of trees that it has the look of an arboretum. An old cemetery stands next to the 10th tee, a reminder of the days when the land was a family farm.

The course has its own covered wooden bridge, spanning water that lies in front of the 13th tee. And between the 7th and 8th fairways a bronze plaque explains a bit of colonial American history for those who have a moment to ponder it. So, even before you tee up a ball, you're in store for some history, plenty of natural beauty, and a touch of old-fashioned New England.

Then, there's the golf, which features a wide variety of good holes that do a good job of following the landscape and avoiding both the monotony and the trick-type holes often found on public golf courses. This isn't to say that the Exeter course doesn't have its weaker holes, but even those can be interesting.

For example, people might criticize the 12th for being too short at 330 yards from the white tees and downhill to boot, but if you play it often enough you come to realize that the hole is not without its own particular guile. Consider that the hole doglegs slightly to the right, but the fairway also slopes to the right, and players who try to cut the corner can find themselves in a world of trouble behind trees and up against a fence on the right side. But if you play a tee shot too far to the left, it can get hung up in trees that can cost you a clear approach. Played strategically, it's the easiest hole on the course, but it can hurt you if you stray.

The next hole, #13, is in the same category. It is even shorter at 310 yards, and it doglegs hard to the left over the last 100 yards or so. But unlike a lot of short, sharp doglegs, this one allows an ambitious player room to gamble – and also room to get in trouble. Either way, the tee shot over both the pond and the aforementioned covered bridge is never uninteresting, especially on those days when someone in the foursome provides the entertainment of rattling a drive around the interior of the bridge. And even the best played drive leaves a testing approach to an uphill green that is bordered on either side by trees.

The toughest hole by far is #7, 420-yard uphill trek that can play into the wind. On the Scratch card, it is a Par-4 and the number-one handicap hole on the front side. Needless to say, the Fair Par cards allow extra shots here to both Level 1 and Level 2 players.

The back nine features a Scratch Par-3 hole, #17, which Level 1 players are allowed to treat as a Par-4, and here's why. The hole measures 200 yards or so from the white tees, but it can play into the wind, and its elevated tee, while helpful in theory, can actually contribute to errant an tee shot's going farther off line than the same shot would if played from a lower tee. It's a hole on which few recreational players make three, and many make five, six or worse. Adding the extra stroke for Level 1 players is aimed at encouraging them to realize they will be far better off to hit the ball straight and in a safe place, even if that place is a little short of the green, than to try to really smack the ball and risk spraying it off line.

In other words, players should resist the urge to hit a wood here. A long iron might not always get you onto the green, but if you're a little short and in the fairway, you still have a fighting chance of chipping on and making three. If you spray a wood into trouble, the fight could be to avoid making having to write an "X" on your card in a place where, at worst, you should be writing a 4.

Fenner Hill Golf Club

33 Wheeler Lane, Hopkington – 539-8000 – 18 holes

Scratch Par – 72
Fair Par Level 1 – 82
Fair Par Level 2 – 93

This lively 18-hole track, built on the hillside site of former farm, opened on Memorial Day weekend, 1999, and it was a welcome addition to the expanding collection of southern Rhode Island public golf courses. Measuring 6,263 yards from the white tees, it is hardly a long course, but it is loaded with character and interesting, challenging golf holes.

The course's overriding feature, and the one that dictates much of its character, is the geological rise that gives the course its name, Fenner Hill. The course's layout sets the majority of the holes climbing, diving, or cutting sideways across the hill's slopes and undulations. In fact, there are only a handful of holes, most on the back nine, where the hill doesn't exert its influence on the flow of play. And although logic and physics tells us that there must be an equal number of ups and downs in our travel from the clubhouse at the first hole back to the same clubhouse at the last hole, many a golfer is likely to leave Fenner Hill GC thinking the demands of having to play uphill exceeded the luxuries of playing downhill.

The potential culprit here is also one of the signature elements of the course: a number of the greens stand above the fairway, and on some of those uphill approaches, the greens are guarded in front by climbing terraces of bunkers. In addition, a majority of the greens have their perimeters defined by grassy mounds, which makes it impossible to run an approach shot along the fairway and onto the greens. Instead, players are required to hit balls on the fly to putting surfaces that they don't have a good view of.

Also, notable on this course are the "environmentally sensitive areas," which are marked and posted. These are the result of an arrangement between the course owners and the state environmental regulators, and are designed to protect wild plant and animal habitats. Golfers are instructed that, not only are they not supposed to play any ball that might land in these areas, they are not allowed to even walk into the areas to search for their balls. Players must treat shots played into these areas as if they were balls lost in the middle of a hazard.

Also notable is the strong contrast between the front and back nines, particularly when it comes to the Scratch Par-4 holes. On the front, these five holes measure in the range of 350-400 yards, and, for the most part, players have a good view from the tee of what lies ahead and where they ought to be playing. Their five counterparts on the back side, however, include not only the three shortest Scratch Par-4s on the course, but also the two longest and, by far, most difficult. Of the short ones, #15 is only 309 yards long and #17 is 297 yards, yet players can't see either green from the tee. As for the long ones, #12 is a straight-away 440-yard brute, and #18, at 425 yards, is easily the most difficult hole on the course, playing over a fairway that is both uphill and side-hill, to an uphill, severely sloping green.

As for the Fair Par ratings here, players are allowed 10 shots over Scratch Par at Level 1 and 21 shots at Level 2. A good example of how those extra shots are designed to help golfers play intelligently can be found on the 3rd hole at Level 1. Here, we have a Scratch Par-5 that, at 486 yards, is relatively short, and it plays downhill, which makes it even shorter. The tendency for an ambitious player, therefore, might be to try to really bang a drive and put himself in position to get home in two shots.

But this is also a treacherous hole, for the narrow, bending fairway is lined with woods on the left, and there is also a fairway bunker on the left that can be in play off the tee. The approach to the green is also tightly guarded by trees and bunkers, and trying to be too aggressive with either the drive or second shot can lead to big trouble. The smart and strategic play for a player here is to hit a club from the tee that he can reliably put in the fairway – a 3- or 4-iron, perhaps – and then hit the same club on the second shot. The result, more often than not, will be a very short, third shot to the green and great chance for a good score.

Foster Country Club

67 Johnson Road, Foster - 397-7750 – 18 holes

Scratch Par - 72 men, 74 women
Fair Par Level 1 – 80
Fair Par Level 2 – 94

Another in the state's list of attractive backcountry golf courses, Foster Country Club is well off the beaten path in the southwestern part of this decidedly rural town, only a few miles from the Connecticut state line.

That it is a former farm turned golf course is plainly evident in the large old barn that stands behind the clubhouse and serves as a maintenance and storage area. And between the 2nd and 4th holes, parallel stands of white pines grow along each side of the old pathway leading to a former family cemetery, where generations of farmers have been laid to rest.

The farm's conversion to golf has been accomplished with some nice touches, particularly the handsomely designed, covered wooden bridge that spans a stream on the 5th hole, and several smaller timber bridges here and there that are designed along the same architectural lines as the covered bridge.

Like a number of other country courses in the state, Foster CC is laid out over two distinct types of landscape: a lowland area, which is fairly open and level, and includes the entire front nine and the final three holes; and an interior that cuts through dense woods and rises and falls over rugged terrain, and includes holes 10 through 15.

If the course has a drawback, it is that there are a number of very short holes played as Scratch Par-4s, and there are also four holes configured in dramatically sharp left-hand doglegs. But there are also a number of very attractive holes that provide a good test of golf.

Leading off the latter category is the 3rd hole, a 241-yard Scratch Par-3 that plays to an uphill green. Immediately next to it, but going in the opposite direction is the very long 4th, a nearly 600-yard monster that plays from an elevated tee, into a wide valley, and back up through a line of trees to the second half of the fairway.

Things ease up on the short #5 hole, but players are immediately tested again on #6, which might be the best hole on the course. At the least it offers the most interesting approach.

The number-one handicap hole, the 6th measures 425 yards and is wide enough to allow players to let out a little shaft from the tee. And any extra distance you can get will be needed if you hope to take only two shots to reach the putting surface, which is a difficult target at best.

Pear-shaped and not particularly big, the green is built like a small shelf on top of a hill, and it falls away steeply in several directions at the edges. As with the 4th hole, Fair Par allows players at both Level 1 and Level 2 an extra shot here.

Two holes on the back nine also qualify for allowances for players at both levels of Fair Par. The first is the 10th, which measures 410 yards and requires a second shot over a hill to a green that, in most cases, players can't see. The second is the 12th, which measures 495 yards and breaks into a nearly 90-degree dogleg left almost directly in front of the tee. The remainder of the hole continues through a chute of trees to a green that is fronted by a stream.

One of the most unusual holes is #13. At 375 yards, the fairway is a rough-and-tumble landscape, punctuated by a nasty chasm that cuts into the fairway about 150 yards from the green. The Fair Par card sets Par at 5 here for both Level 1 and Level 2.

Foxwoods Golf & Country Club at Boulder Hills

87 Kingstown Road (Rt. 138), Richmond – 539-4653 – 18 holes

Scratch Par – 70
Fair Par Level 1 – 78
Fair Par Level 2 – 92

A very young track, this golf course has already gone through the kind of changes that many courses don't see in a lifetime.

One is that almost immediately after being opened in 1995, the 18th hole became the 1st hole, as the course was reconfigured to allow construction of a practice range.

Another is that in 1997, the Pequot Indian Tribe, owners of Foxwoods Casino in nearby Connecticut, gained a substantial financial interest in the property, which had been owned exclusively by a Providence-based investment group.

And with the change in ownership came a change in name, from the original, Boulder Hills, to one that also incorporates the name of the casino.

Whatever the wisdom of the business deal, there was a bit of a downside to changing the name, for few golf courses have ever been characterized so succinctly as this one was when it was called simply Boulder Hills.

There are so many boulders and so many hills here, in fact, it's a wonder anyone ever undertook the project of building a course on this site in the first place.

Yet, here it stands, a rolling and rock-strewn test of golf that some have criticized as being too punitive – that is, there is too much of a penalty to pay for making mistakes. Drives that stray from the fairway, for example, often land not in grassy rough, but in rocky terrain that can send the ball pinging away in directions unknown.

The loudest complainers, of course, are likely to be those players who insist on trying to hit the ball too hard, particularly off the tee, and who don't recognize that keeping the ball in the fairway – here, as at most golf courses – should be a player's first priority.

On the other hand, players who take the principles of Fair Par play to heart are likely to enjoy themselves here, for with all the rugged terrain come some interesting and unique vantages: elevated tees, shots over valleys, fairways that climb and dive like ski slopes.

The fact is, from the white tees this course is fairly short, only a shade over 5,600 yards at a Scratch Par of 70. Keep the ball in the fairway and you'll be fine.

Local knowledge is almost a must here, principally because the terrain creates a large number of blind tee shots and even blind second shots that must be made over hills that block a player's view of the landing area.

In addition, the slopes in some of the landing areas are tricky and can send the ball scooting into tough spots if you happen to land it in the wrong place. Or, the slopes are such that you are sometimes better to hit shorter to a flatter landing area, rather than longer to a place where the next shot will be from a side-hill stance.

Bottom line: until you know the course yourself, you'll have more fun if you play with someone who has been there before.

As for Fair Par, Level 1 players get four shots over Scratch Par on the front nine and five shots over Scratch on the back, making a Level 1 Fair Par of 79. Level 2 players get 11 shots on each nine, for a Fair Par 92. The two levels share breaks on the front at hole #3, 420 yards long, and #4, a 465 yarder that plays along a rolling, uphill fairway and requires, in many cases, a blind second shot over a hill to the green.

On the back, both levels get extra strokes at the 398-yard 14th, where the fairway hardly has a flat spot, and the 415-yard 16th, which requires that a blind tee shot be played down hill to a narrow landing area.

Goddard Memorial State Park

Ives Road, Warwick – 884-9834 – 9 holes

Scratch Par for 18 holes – 72
Fair Par Level 1 – 80
Fair Par Level 2 – 94

Part of the state's sprawling Goddard Park complex, this 9-hole track has been a workhorse of public play for decades.

Many an older golfer in Rhode Island can remember playing his first round at this course, when it cost less than a dollar for nine holes, and when yardage markers consisted of red metal poles planted at the edges of the fairway to indicate you had traveled 200 yards from the tee.

Even today, the greens fees are among the lowest anywhere, attracting legions of retired, fixed-income players and other cost-conscious golfers, all of whom get a glimpse, as they walk to the 5th tee, of how the more well-heeled folk live – for there, a wedge shot away, stands the lush, private Potowomut Golf Club.

You get what you pay for, of course, and the result is that the playing conditions at Goddard are often not good, particularly in the fairways, where grass can be a scarce commodity by the time August rolls around. That aside, you can pay plenty more at other courses for layouts that are less challenging, and less interesting.

The first hole, for example, starts the nine off in anything but a pushover fashion, for it measures 500 yards and can play into the wind on a summer afternoon.

The 2nd hole, at 375 yards, demands that you hit a drive either over or around a large spreading tree, and on the second shot players must contend with a yawning bunker at the front left of the green. And #3, at 185 yards, is far from an easy hole to negotiate in 3 shots.

The weakest hole on the course is the short, straight 4th, but the 5th returns the challenge to players, as it measures 496 yards and requires a blind tee shot that must travel over a hill and, often, into the wind.

The 6th, a sharp left-hand dogleg, is a cakewalk for a player who can hook the ball, but it plays much longer for the sort of players the course tends to attract: golfers whose predominant tendencies are to hit tee shots from left to right.

The next hole is an uncomplicated but solid Scratch Par-3 that leads, in turn, to the toughest hole on the course, the 390-yard 8th, which plays into the wind in the summer and features an undulating fairway that can result in less roll on a drive and an awkward stance for the second shot.

The nine finishes with a Par-4 that is straight, wide, and, at 321 yards, a fairly easy hole.

When you're done with a round at Goddard, a glance at your scorecard likely will reveal that you hardly have played the easiest nine holes in the state (an idea confirmed by the fact that Fair Par Level 1 is 80 and Level 2 is 94).

Another glance into your wallet will indicate that you've just experienced the golfing equivalent of a bargain.

And if that's not enough, you can always drive a short way down the road and put in an application for membership at Potowomut.

Green Valley Country Club

371 Union Street, Portsmouth – 847-9543 – 18 holes

Scratch Par – 71
Fair Par Level 1 – 83
Fair Par Level 2 – 95

Which is the most challenging public golf course in Rhode Island? Put that question to the state's golfers and you're sure to get plenty of votes for Green Valley.

At 6,641 yards from the white tees and 6,830 from the blues, it is easily longer than the large majority of the state's courses, public or private, from any tee you want to name.

And that's at a Scratch Par of 71.

Granted, the greens are hardly as slick and tricky as you might find, say, a few miles away at Wanumetonomy (a private track), or down the road at Newport CC (another private course).

But the trials of simply getting to the greens are what give Green Valley its well-deserved reputation as a course that puts serious demands on the recreational golfer.

Also well-deserved is the praise that has been accorded over the years to Manuel Raposa, who farmed the land, until one day he decided to plant putting greens in place of potatoes.

The distances Green Valley asks a player to travel become evident rather quickly – on the second hole, in fact, which is listed on the Scratch card as a 454-yard Par 4. Two holes later comes the Scratch Par-5, 541-yard 5th.

But the true, brutal character of the course doesn't show itself until a little farther along, when players have descended into the long, green valley that gives the place its name. Actually, it's a nice valley, so long as your direction of travel is downhill. The problem comes when you are asked to play your way back up.

That difficult task begins at #8, an uphill 201-yard Scratch Par-3. The travail continues to an even more difficult extent at #9, which runs 424-yards uphill and is rated a Scratch Par-4. If you could count on a trailing wind on these two holes, things might not seem so tough, but the prevailing summer breeze is almost always a hindrance, if not an outright enemy.

The 10th hole, at 605 yards from the white tees, is the longest on the course and one of the longest in the state. It is some comfort that the hole heads downhill, back into the valley, but that's still a pile of yards.

Nor is there any relief in the next hole, a fairly level but long Scratch Par-3, 220 yards in length.

Players can relax a little on the next two holes, but by #14, it's time to muscle up again and try to cover 440 yards in four shots, according to the Scratch card.

And if you think that was a test, two holes later comes the 540-yard 17th, which plays uphill and dead into the prevailing southwesterly summer breeze – and is further complicated by a little bend to the right and some well-placed fairway bunkers.

It goes without saying that Fair Par is crucial for the recreational player at Green Valley, if for no better reason than to keep his spirits up on a hot July day, when trudging up through that verdant valley over all those yards can make a person question his motives for pursuing such a pastime.

In fact, the Level 1 Fair Par at Green Valley is 83, the highest of any of the state's public courses. And at 95, the Level 2 Fair Par is exceeded only by Montaup's 96 and Trigg's 97, among the state's 18-hole public courses.

Jamestown Golf Course

245 Conanicus Ave., Jamestown – 423-9930 – 9 holes

Scratch Par for 18 holes – 72 men, 76 women
Fair Par Level 1 – 80
Fair Par Level 2 – 94

Situated smack in the middle of Conanicut Island, better known as Jamestown, this 9-hole track, established in 1895, is a backyard favorite for island residents and a convenient stop for summer tourists looking to play a quick nine between the morning sail and the cocktails and steamers in the evening.

If you spend enough time in this island town, sooner or later you will be impressed with the wonderful sense of community that pervades the place. It is a very small island, after all, and residents run into one another every day as they shop in the island's few retail stores, eat in the town's handful of restaurants, and stop at the only two gas stations.

Golfers have that sense of community to thank for the fact that there still is a Jamestown Golf Course at all, for there was a time during the real estate boom of the 1980s when the course's future was very much in doubt. Developers had cast a covetous eye on the place, envisioning condos, townhouses, and upscale single-family homes. And the course's owner was ready to sell. But island pride and community spirit would not abide that. We might not all be golfers, island activists said, but we love our island and all that open green space in the middle that the golf course provides. They argued that the course was a refuge for the wildlife that dwelled in the overgrown edges of the course, and that it was also a refuge for residents during the peace and quiet of the winter, when the snow was on the ground and the golfers had put away their sticks until the spring.

It was a message that islanders took to heart, and a proposal was made that the town would buy the course to keep it out of the hands of developers. The Town Council decided to let the town's voters decide the issue: Should the town – meaning its taxpayers – fork over $2 million to save the golf course? When the vote was held, there was no doubt, as voters declared overwhelmingly, "No condos. We want the golf course!"

And the town has owned the course since, leasing it to private managers.

As for the quality of golf the course offers, the place is about an even mix of holes that can boost your golfing ego and holes that can make you realize that your game needs more work. The one thing almost all the holes have in common is that they are wide open from the tees, which means that this is a golf course where players can work on trying to put a little more power into the driver, while knowing that there will be a smaller penalty for spraying the ball than at some other courses.

The tougher tests on the course tend to be the even-numbered holes, beginning with #2, a 541-yard travel, whose fairway slopes to the right toward a pond that has caught many a sliced tee shot over the years.

The 4th, at 388 yards, is a very good driving hole, running downhill and downwind in the prevailing summer breeze. But the second shot can be tricky and requires the local knowledge that counsels players to land the approach well short of the green, for it will feed downhill rapidly. Many an approach on this hole will look perfect, only to end up bounding over the green, whose back edge falls away steeply to the rough below. To make things even trickier, the green is very small and a maze of hard-to-read slopes.

The 6th, measuring 450 yards, isn't long for a Scratch Par-5, but it almost always plays straight into the wind in the summer. And coming back the other way is the 8th, which offers similar driving advantages as #4, and also some of the same difficulties at the green. In this case, however, the green has the unusual feature of being divided into two tiers along its length – that is, the left hand side of the narrow putting surface, from front to back, is a step below the right hand side.

It is anything but an easy Par-4, which is why Fair Par Level 1 players are allowed 5 shots, and Level 2 players are granted 6 blows to make Par here.

Laurel Lane Golf Course

309 Laurel Lane, West Kingston – 783-3844 – 18 holes

Scratch Par – 71 men, 70 women
Fair Par Level 1 – 79
Fair Par Level 2 – 92

Like Green Valley, Laurel Lane is an example of how a family of farmers can convert its cash crop from potatoes or corn to golf.

That is exactly what the Holley family did back in 1960s with the family spread that they and others before them had farmed for decades along the banks of the Queens River. The result was a track that will never be mistaken for a world class course, but one that, nevertheless, proved successful enough that the Holleys were able to sell the operation in 1996 for a lot more than small potatoes. Under new ownership, the course got some needed additions, including a practice range that was cut into the woods next to the 18th hole, and it continues to be a busy operation.

As you play the course, it is not difficult to imagine where most of the farming took place, for there are two distinct types of terrain – the flat, wide open lowlands that include the first four holes, a place where plowing and planting would have been easy, and the more rugged uplands, where there are several holes that had to be hacked out of the woods.

There is also a great variety to the holes among the course's 18, ranging from very easy to very difficult, and from traditional in look and shape to highly idiosyncratic, requiring plenty of local knowledge in order to avoid courting disaster.

The best pure golf holes on the course are probably the two Scratch Par-5s on the back side. The 11th measures 462 yards, and features an elevated tee and an undulating fairway that slopes to the left while curving gradually to the right along a line of woods. The green, severely sloped in places, is set on a rise and amid trees, and it not only can be a tough target, but also tough to putt when you get there. Overall, it is not easy to make five here, so Level 1 players are allowed six shots and Level 2 players get seven.

54

More difficult still is the 13th. At 528 yards, it plays into the prevailing summer breeze, through a chute of tall trees, over a substantial pond that lies about halfway to the hole, and then up a hill to a severely sloped green. It is a hole that recreational players tend to play in seven, eight, or worse far more often than they make five, and the Fair Par for the hole compensates for that at both Levels 1 and 2.

One interesting aspect of Fair Par at Laurel Lane is that the shortest Scratch Par-4 hole on the course, #6, is rated at 5 shots on the Level 1 card – and there are good reasons. The hole measures only 245 yards, but the first two-thirds of it play over a long slender pond. After that, the fairway climbs in uneven terraces to a difficult, hilltop green. To the left and right of the green, the hill falls away drastically toward the forest.

The extra shot at Level 1 is aimed at discouraging players at this level from pulling out the driver and trying to bang it at the green. A stray No. 1 wood on this hole can be a quick ticket to disaster – and a driver struck with the kind of over-swing that playing over a pond can induce is an invitation to lift the head and top the golf ball into the drink. On the other hand, a strategic long iron over the pond will put a player safely on the hillside below the green, just a soft pitch shot from the putting surface.

One quick aside: Anyone who hasn't played Laurel Lane in recent years will notice a big change (among several, less drastic alterations) when they reach the 5th hole. There, lay one of the course's trademarks: a muddy pond (called Blue's Bog) and a tall, lone pine tree set in the left center of the fairway, within a long hitter's driving distance from the tee.

Together, they were a somewhat odd occurrence of hazards, and not to everyone's liking, for they seemed to artificially constrict the fairway to a narrow gateway on the right side. But they also served to give the short hole, a Scratch Par-4 at 315 yards, some memorable character. For better or worse, both the tree and the bog are gone, replaced with a fairway bunker and a diagonal line of small mounds.

Meadow Brook Golf Course

Route 138, Richmond – 539-8491 – 18 holes

Scratch Par – 71 men, 73 women
Fair Par Level 1 – 79
Fair Par Level 2 – 90

A former colonial-era farm hard by Route 138, this is as unpretentious and laid-back a golf course as you'll find anywhere in the state – so much so that it has not been uncommon for the course to operate without a starter.

That's right, golf on the honor system. You put your money in an envelope, drop the envelope through a slot into a collection box, and away you go.

Needless to say, there's no valet parking. No obsequious clubhouse boys rushing over to haul your bags from your car and call you "sir" or "ma'am" as often as possible. No gallery of past club presidents hung up on the clubhouse wall like trophy game. No grill room.

Just golf. Inexpensive, unadorned, country golf.

Naturally, such a system hardly allows for the sort of maintenance budget that will keep the course looking like Augusta National on a Masters weekend, but that doesn't mean you can't enjoy yourself on the golf course, and plenty of people do, year round.

The fact is that, although the course has some weak holes (as most courses do), the layout offers some very good and interesting golf. And even among the weaker holes, there are redeeming qualities.

Take the first hole, for example. On the scorecard it might not look like much, but it offers exactly what any civilized opening hole should: forgiveness. A chance to get going on your round without a struggle. A short, uncomplicated, user-friendly introduction to your day of golf.

Also on the front side, players find two of the best holes on the golf course, beginning with the 5th, which plays 155 yards from an elevated tee, over a big pond, and down to lovely green. From tee to green the hole is set in an amphitheater of trees.

Then comes the 6th, easily the most interesting hole on the course.

56

At 535 yards and heavily wooded on both sides, it is less a dogleg and more a long sweeping crescent, bending seemingly forever to the right.

As players get within hailing distance of the green, the fairway funnels into a narrow canyon created by a bank of large mounds bordering the left side of the fairway. At last, the green appears, tucked back under tall, overarching trees.

Like Laurel Lane and other country courses that were former farms, Meadow Brook plays alternately through level, lowland areas, that once would have been the most conducive to growing crops, and through more rugged, rocky wooded terrain on higher ground.

But there is a surprise in store here on the back nine, which begins in the lowlands, winds into the woods, and suddenly, behind the 13th green, opens into a second, broad level area.

At the 385-yard 15th, that same wide, flat terrain creates the best driving hole on the golf course, an expanse of fairway that begs players to let their inhibitions loose on the tee. In fact, the hole's length might qualify it as a 5-stroke hole at Level 1 Fair Par, but the inviting driving area means that the rating stays at Par-4, encouraging players, as John Daly would say, to "grip it and rip it."

Melody Hill Golf Course

Sawmill Road, Harmony – 949-9851 – 18 holes

Scratch Par – 71
Fair Par Level 1 – 80
Fair Par Level 2 – 93

On the official scorecard, this golf course is billed as "The Beautiful Melody Hill." And in many places along this backcountry, 18-hole track, that glowing description is well deserved, for the course winds through the hills and woods of Harmony, offering lovely views of the country.

That this course is former farm is evident from the moment you pull into the parking lot, for looming up on the right is a mammoth barn, which now does duty as the clubhouse, pro shop, and maintenance and storage shed.

At Fair Par Level 2, Melody Hill is unique among the state's courses, because the front nine features two holes on which the Level 2 rating is the same as the Scratch Par.

The first of these is #4, a 95-yard Par-3 that is simply too short and offers too little trouble of any kind to be made into a Par-4, even at Level 2.

(As an aside, the hole also features a very large bunker that is positioned rather cruelly, on the left side of the fairway, some 20 yards short of the front edge of the green, which means it is set up to penalize the sort of player who is unable to advance the ball more than 50 or 60 yards from the tee, and who has pulled it left to boot. A heartless penalty, indeed!)

The second of the Level 2 anomalies is the 8th hole, a straight, wide, 235-yarder that is complicated only by the presence of a large pine guarding the front right of the green. The Scratch card sets the Par at 4, and there seems little reason to alter that, even at Level 2.

If Melody Hill is anything, it is unpredictable. For example, on the front side, the pitch-and-putt tameness of #4 is followed immediately by the extravagance of #5, a 465-yard piece of drama that dives left and downward, through an alley of trees, with the steepness of ski slope.

That is followed by the elegant 6th hole, which plays 145 yards from an uphill tee down to a green framed on the left and right by trees, and in the background by a tree-lined pond that lies on the edge of the 7th fairway.

Both #7 and #8 are strong holes, particularly the latter, which is friendly at first, offering a wide inviting driving area, but then turns tough, as the fairway sweeps left toward the hole. At the same time, the fairway slopes decidedly to the right toward dense woods.

The back side also includes some very good holes, as well as a roller coaster finish, with #16 doglegging and diving hard downhill, #17 bending back uphill, and #18 falling again, leaving players to putt out in the shadow of Melody Hill's giant barn.

Midville Country Club

100 Lombardi Lane, West Warwick – 828-9215 – 9 holes

Scratch Par for 18 holes – 70
Fair Par Level 1 – 77
Fair Par Level 2 – 90

The credit for the creation of the lovely Midville Country Club goes to Carmine Lombardi, although it isn't clear whether he should be congratulated for designing a golf course surrounded by a garden, or a garden that just happens to have a golf course running through it.

Either way, one of Midville's most pleasant attributes is that it resembles a carefully tended floral garden built on a large scale, one that artfully mixes well-planned plantings with the natural elements and contours of the terrain.

The result is a golf course that is easy on the senses, and, it turns out, relatively easy on the average player's golf game.

In other words, if you want a day of golf filled with brutal challenges, and the frustrations that come with them, play somewhere else. On the other hand, if you want to work on your game without having to grind all day, and if one of your reasons for playing is simply to get outside and enjoy the scenery, then you will like Midville.

One other of the course's attributes is that it does something not all 9-hole tracks do: it encourages golfers playing 18 holes to play the first round from the white tees and the second round from the blues.

The change adds less than 200 yards to the length of the course (2,779 yards from the white, 2,970 from the blue), but it can mean playing different shots with different clubs on several of the holes, thus adding variety to the game.

It also adds strokes to the Level 1 Fair Par rating, which is 37 from the white tees and 40 from the blue. Depending on how you look at it, then, it might be advantageous for Level 1 players to start the round from the blue tees, given the fact that, even with the added yardage, the addition of the three strokes on Par could make a player more comfortable from the blues.

Then, with 9 holes under your belt, you might be better prepared for the more exacting 37-stroke standard from the shorter tees. It's your call.

Regardless of which tees you decide on, however, you should be happy with the first hole, for it offers the very thing players need on an opening hole, particularly if they haven't had a good chance to warm up: a relatively short hole with a wide driving area.

The only trick here, however, is to avoid the tall tree that stands about in the middle of the fairway and that can catch drives that aren't hit high enough.

The second hole is one of the shortest but also one of the most interesting holes on the course. It measures only 321 yards from the blue tees and 314 from the whites, but it features a pond on the right about half-way to the green, and a fairway that bends a little to the right.

A line of trees pinches in from the left, and more trees on the right form a bit of a corner to the fairway as it rises to the green. The green itself is guarded by a bunker in front on the right and a large mound at the left front.

So, the drive must be hit carefully to avoid straying into either the pond or the trees, and then the approach to the green must be made on the fly, as there is little chance to run it up. But beware, for almost immediately behind the green stand a stonewall and a fence that leave virtually no room for shots that are played too long.

The longest, toughest, and best hole on the course is #6, which plays between 523 and 540 yards slightly downhill, over an undulating fairway, from a tee that commands long views of the landscape beyond the golf course.

The 7th, at 171 yards, is also a very nice hole, again offering long vistas from a high tee before playing over a small valley to a green surrounded by large, spreading trees.

Montaup Country Club

Anthony Road, Portsmouth – 683-9107 – 18 holes

Scratch Par – 71 men, 73 women
Fair Par Level 1 – 81
Fair Par Level 2 – 96

Even on a calm day, golfers surely would rank Montaup as one of the more challenging of the state's public courses. But add the breezes that blow almost constantly here, from one direction and another, and there is no doubt.

How could it not be windy? The course is not only located on an island (Aquidneck), it is situated at the island's northern tip, between Mt. Hope Bay on one side, and Sakonnet River (which should be called Sakonnet Bay for it is not a river at all) on the other. And just as the salt water rushes through the channel between Aquidneck Island and the Tiverton mainland, so the wind dashes over the water through channels of its own, bringing Montaup much of its golfing character.

For better or worse, Montaup wastes no time in issuing its challenge to those who have come to play it, for it features the sort of opening hole that can make an unprepared player question how he has chosen to spend his afternoon. The 1st measures 398 yards from the white tees, over a somewhat narrow, left-sloping fairway – not an easy driving hole, and that's a problem, because a long straight drive is crucial here to finding comfort on the approach.

The big problem on the second shot is a pond that lies directly in front and to the right of the green. If the second shot doesn't end up on the green here, chances are good that it has found trouble. It's a hole that recreational golfers tend to play in 6 shots or worse more often than they play it in 4, and for that reason it is one of four holes on the front side and three on the back on which players at both Fair Par Level 1 and Level 2 are allowed extra shots.

The 2nd hole plays about the same length as the first, albeit without the problematic pond, and the 3rd is a 211-yard Scratch Par-3. The length moderates after that for the remainder of the nine, but the character of the holes remains strong. On the 5th, for example, after clearing a pond at the corner of a slight left hand dogleg, players encounter the well-bunkered green, which rises just enough to do two things: make the approach less than a cinch, and offer players their best view so far of Mt. Hope Bay.

The short but pretty #8 hole plays 137 yards over a pond to a skinny, well-bunkered green. And #9, although only 325 yards long, adds a severely undulating fairway to the equation.

The back nine starts benignly with a straight, friendly 148-yard Par-3, but it is followed quickly by a completely different experience: the 394-yard 11th, a dogleg left, smack on the shore of Mt. Hope Bay. One way or another, the wind is almost always a big factor here, as is the green, which is sloped steeply from back to front.

The course heads back inland again before returning to the shore on the tame-looking, but potentially treacherous 16th. At only 445 yards and a Scratch Par 5, it would seem short on the scorecard, but there are two potential problems: the wind, and a pond that lurks, almost unseen, in a depression just in front and to the right of the green. If the wind direction is right and you can avoid the pond, this could be the easiest hole on the golf course. If the wind is wrong, and you forget about the pond, the outcome can be quite different.

The 17th is memorable for a couple of reasons. The first is the tee shot, which must be played over a tiny, historic cemetery. The second is the approach shot, which must be played to a skinny green that is tucked against a line of evergreen trees on the left and then falls away sharply on the right.

And, as if to say to golfers, "You've suffered enough," the last hole, at only 293 yards, allows players to coast home and, perhaps, finish feeling good about themselves after some of the problems they no doubt encountered earlier.

North Kingstown Golf Course

Callahan Road, Davisville – 294-4051 – 18 holes

Scratch Par – 70
Fair Par Level 1 – 79
Fair Par Level 2 – 91

This golf course was originally built by the federal government as part of the sprawling Quonset Point Naval Air Station, and, for the years it was in government hands, it was poorly cared for and lacked a good irrigation system, so it tended to resemble a hayfield by July.

In the years following the war in Vietnam, it began to look as if Quonset was not in the Navy's long-term plans. As the base's closing finally became reality, the town stepped, took over the course, and turned it into a municipal success story. The town has made an especially good effort to improve maintenance, and the result is that golfers can now enjoy the course for what it always was: a pretty solid golf layout.

Remnants of the golf course's military heritage are still evident in places, particularly on the back nine, as the 13th hole leads players to the edge of what used to be the air station's airport.

Although the airport is owned by the state today, it is home to a local Air National Guard group, which means the airfield still has a pronounced military look to it.

If the course has one shortcoming that the town's ownership couldn't fix, it is a relative sameness in elevation. The fairways, for the most part, are level and there is a near absence of the elevated tees or greens that can add drama to a golf landscape.

But the course has almost everything else a player could want, and even the shorter holes have character. The 154-yard 3rd, for example, plays over a pond. The 5th, at 362 yards, plays through a kind of pinched-waist in the fairway, where trees, lining a stream, close in from both the left and right in an area that many players might be landing their drives.

The 343-yard 6th doglegs over water and low trees, and invites bigger hitters to take chances. Even the very short 9th, at only 276 yards, is interesting in that the green is virtually hidden behind bunkers.

The 12th is short at 321 yards, but it plays over a small pond from a pretty teeing area to a well-bunkered green. And the 304-yard 17th is distinguished by several very large spreading trees that create a dogleg left and force a strategic tee shot to the right if the approach is to have a good chance.

The best and toughest hole on the golf course is probably the 15th, a 403-yard dogleg right that presents players with a challenging tee shot, which, in turn, can determine whether the approach has any chance of getting to the green in good shape.

The tee is set behind a pond, which, itself, lies at the bottom of a rise in the fairway. Dense woods border the pond and form the corner of the dogleg on the right. A line of more sparsely planted but still problematic trees borders the left hand edge of the fairway. Add to all that the fact that the prevailing summer breeze is often in your face on the tee, and that the green, when you eventually get it in sight, lies behind a bunch of ugly bunkers.

In short, a player faces more than 400 yards, over a pond, uphill, into the wind, through trees, around a dogleg, and into a green whose access is heavily guarded by bunkers.

It's no surprise that the hole gets the top handicap rating on the back side, and that Fair Par players at both Level 1 and Level 2 are allowed extra shots on #15.

Pocasset Country Club

807 Bristol Ferry Road, Portsmouth – 683-7300 – 9 holes

Scratch Par for 18 holes – 68 men, 70 women
Fair Par Level 1 – 76
Fair Par Level 2 – 88

Pocasset is a modest but interesting 9-hole track that lies almost in the shadow of the Mt. Hope Bridge and just down the road from its better known cousin, Montaup.

As at Montaup, the wind blowing off Mount Hope Bay and Sakonnet River can be an important element of play here, although none of the holes on the course actually border the shore.

There is another natural element here, however, that provides a lovely and unusual aspect to the course: the acres of tall marsh grasses that grow in a wetland that abuts the course along the 7th and 8th holes. So dense are the plants that they literally form a waving wall of stalks and fuzzy tops, and although they never come into play, they are memorable nonetheless.

The course is an odd mix of holes that, on the Scratch card, include no Par-5s and three Par-4s that measure 300 yards or less, but also a 425-yard uphill Par-4 and a pair of tough Par-3 holes measuring 195 and 210 yards.

The course is set on a broad hillside, and first hole plays uneventfully, 305 yards downward, with a nice view of the course and landscape beyond in the background.

At the green, one of the prevailing characteristics of the course appears: a putting surface that is level with the fairway at the front, but built up and dropping off sharply in the back, which means that approach shots hit too far leave players with much more difficult chips and pitches to the green than shots that might be hit too short.

The first of the two Scratch Par-3s is the 3rd, which measures 210 yards to a small, narrow green that, like so many others on the course, falls off at the back and also on the right. It is also complicated by a green-side bunker on the left and another bunker that lies some 20 yards or so in front of the green.

The other Par-3 is #6, 195 yards downhill to a green that falls away to the left, right, and back even more severely than the rest. Worse still, a water hazard lies little more than a dozen yards or so behind the green – all of which means that hitting a ball over this green is a bad idea.

For those who would be tempted to hit short, however, a fairway bunker is strategically placed 30 yards or so in front of the green.

Players at Fair Par Level 1 are allowed an extra shot on both #3 and #6 to encourage common sense, which means avoiding the temptation to play for the pin on these holes, particularly if that play means hauling a wood out of your bag.

Spraying the ball or hitting it over will cost you shots unnecessarily, particularly on #6. A better thought is to hit a club that can take you to the front edge of each green. If you hit it well, you're on the green. If you don't get it all, you're a little short or, at worst, in the front bunkers playing to a green that is tilted toward you, rather than being to one side or behind, playing from a much worse angle.

Remember, Fair Par is aimed at allowing you to strategically manage *the entire golf course*, without feeling that you need to hit home runs on difficult holes.

Richmond Country Club

74 Sandy Pond Road, Richmond – 364-9200 – 18 holes

Scratch Par – 71
Fair Par Level 1 – 80
Fair Par Level 2 – 93

One of the youngest golf courses in the state, Richmond was cut out the evergreens and hardwoods of the rural countryside. The result, everyone seems to agree, is a handsome, well-kept woodlands course that can play quite differently depending on which tees golfers choose to hit from.

From the white tees, for example, the course measures just over 5,800 yards, and can be played by reasonably good golfers without having (or wanting) to hit the driver too often.

From the blue tees, the course jumps in length by nearly 700 yards, and the championship markers, the gold tees, add 300 more yards, for a total of 6,826.

No matter what markers you play, the course is characterized by medium to narrow fairways that are hemmed in on both sides by woods. The terrain is generally flat, although a number of mounds and undulations have been built into some of the fairways. For the most part, however, there is very little change in elevation from tee to green.

The only substantial water on the course is found on the last hole, where a pond lies on the left and short of the green.

From the white tees, there are a handful of fairly short holes – including, thankfully, the first – but they are not often without character. One of the best examples is the 9th hole, which plays only 285 yards from the white tees and can tempt a player into trouble.

The hole doglegs left for about the final third of its length, and the temptation off the tee is to try to cut the corner closely enough to play almost directly at the green. What lies in wait, however, is a succession of bunkers, marching from the corner of the dogleg almost right up to the green.

The number-one handicap hole on the front side is the 4th, a 504-yard beauty that sweeps gradually but steadily to the right through the bordering thickets of trees. The fairway is never particularly wide, and there is a tendency to hit shots into the trees on the left out of fear of pushing shots into the trees on the right.

Another strong hole is the 6th, which, at 428 yards, is the longest Scratch Par-4 on the course from the white tees. The hole doglegs left, and players trying to cut the corner too closely must contend with a series of bunkers placed there precisely to foil the easy route to the hole.

The back nine features a pair of interesting long holes, both Scratch Par 5s. One is #11, a sweeping, narrow crescent of a hole that bends persistently to the left. Mounds along the right and trees along the left make for difficult decisions about the best strategies to take. In the end, patience pays off, although the temptation to try to cut corners is strong.

Then, there is the 16th, a sharp dogleg right that requires a solid, straight tee shot to clear the corner for a good look at the green. Even then, players are faced with numerous fairway and green-side bunkers, as well as a two-tier green that can be difficult to putt if you end up on the wrong level.

Rolling Greens

Ten Rod Road, North Kingstown – 294-9859 – 9 holes

Scratch Par for 18 holes – 70 men, 74 women
Fair Par Level 1 – 78
Fair Par Level 2 – 92

Rolling Greens is a 9-hole track that, in terms of amenities, has little in common with its more upscale cousin, Exeter Country Club, which lies a few miles farther west along Route 102.

What it does hold in common with Exeter, however, is the availability of interesting golf holes, for with the exception of the benign opening hole, each of the holes on this modest course has something of character to offer.

A decidedly woodland track, with dense stands of mature trees lining most of the fairways, the course begins as all civilized courses should, with a relatively short (339 yards), open hole. It allows golfers, particularly those who haven't gotten themselves sufficiently warmed up, to ease into the round without having their golfing hearts broken right off the bat.

The next hole is only 353 yards long, but the fairway is tight on both sides with trees, making the tee shot somewhat problematic. Although the hole is not long, Fair Par allows Level 1 players an extra shot here to encourage them to keep the ball in the fairway off the tee. Accomplish that, and you will profit, but to spray the tee shot here is to court disaster.

The 3rd hole plays 383 yards over a pond that lies directly in front of the tee. The fairway then rises a bit and undulates, which will reduce the roll a player is likely to get on his tee shot. The uneven fairway also complicates the second shot, because there is a good chance of having some type of side-hill lie.

At only 147 yards, the 4th hole might not look like much on the scorecard, but completing it in three shots isn't easy. The principal problem is that the green resembles a shelf atop a mound, which falls away on nearly all sides, and shots that are hit long and especially to the left can end up in places you don't want to be.

70

The 5th is the best hole on the golf course. At 550 yards, it is not only long, but it offers the most difficult thing a long hole can: a tough tee shot. The fairway is a roller coaster, and its first big climb occurs exactly in the area where many players are likely to land drives. Worse, it has a strong slope to the left that tends to encourage tee balls to run amok down a heavily wooded hillside.

For the player who can survive the trials off the tee, however, the hole offers a reward: a picturesque downhill approach to the green, which is framed by tall trees.

The 6th and 7th are both very short Par-4 holes, but each offers a challenge. The 6th, for example, plays as an uphill left-hand dogleg around a clump of large trees, and big hitters might well be tempted to go straight for the green, only to find that the treetops have nicked the ball and sent it into trouble.

The 7th doglegs left as well, but this hole plays downhill. Again, big hitters are often tempted to hit directly for the green, but trees crowd the fairway from both the left and the right, and being a little off line can bring a lot of trouble.

The 220-yard 8th hole might ordinarily qualify as a Fair Par-4 at Level 1, primarily to encourage players to avoid getting into trouble with a big wood shot off the tee. The difference here is that there is almost no trouble to get into, so the hole plays as a Fair Par-3 and Level 1 players are encouraged to hit the driver or 3-wood if they feel they need it.

The course finishes with the 440-yard 9th, which is wide open, but also plays uphill and often into the wind. For those reasons, it qualifies as a Par-5 at Level 1 and a Par-6 at Level 2.

Seaview Country Club

150 Gray Street, Warwick – 739-6311 – 9 holes

Scratch Par for 18 holes – 72
Fair Par Level 1 – 78
Fair Par Level 2 – 92

Seaview gets it name because several vantages on the golf course offer views of upper Narragansett Bay and of the busy boating activities that occupy the nearby coves in the warm months.

The golf course is often overshadowed by its more prestigious cousin down the road, the private Warwick Country Club, but Seaview should not be overlooked, for it is not only lovely and well-kept, it offers several fine golf holes among its nine.

The course is quite short, measuring only 2,903 yards at a Scratch Par of 36. But distance isn't everything, and nothing is more characteristic of that axiom at Seaview than the opening hole.

The 1st measures only 305 yards and, from the tee, there would appear to be no trouble in store. But there is, for cutting across the fairway with the stealth of a snake is a small stream. It lies roughly two-thirds of the way to the green, and depending on how far and what type of tee shot you make, it can be a factor.

Then, regardless of which side of the stream you end up on, the approach to the green is short but far from easy. First, the green lies well above the fairway, and, second, it is partially fronted by a large, spreading tree that can knock down an approach with ease.

And when you finally get to the green, you discover that it is a two-tiered affair that can be difficult to putt.

Similar scenarios occur at the 7th and 8th. On #7, only 302 yards lie between the tee and the hole, but a tall oak on the left can induce a player to aim his tee shot too far to the right, where a stream and heavy vegetation wait to swallow the ball.

On the 8th, 350 yards long, heavy woods crowd in from the right, and other trees line the left side of the narrow fairway. The fairway also slopes from right to left, so if a player starts his ball too far to the left to avoid the dense woods, the slope is likely to push the ball even further to the left into the trees on that side.

To give a player even more to think about, a large fairway bunker lies entirely across the face of the green, although some 20 yards or so short of it.

The course isn't entirely without length, and most of it comes on the 551-yard 5th, the longest and potentially most difficult hole on the course. The hole is technically a dogleg right, but actually is more one long sweep in that direction.

For the first two-thirds of its length, there is tree trouble along both sides of the fairway. Finally, as you get the green in sight, the trees give way on the right, but can still be a factor on the left, as the fairway tends to slope in that direction.

The approach is complicated by a nasty fairway bunker several dozen yards short of the green and by bunkers at green-side.

One of the best and prettiest holes on the course is the 6th. At 201 yards long, the hole is bordered along its right side by a stream that blossoms into a pond to the right of and behind the green. Along the banks of the waterway, pretty wildflowers and elegant marsh grasses can make the experience of knocking a ball into the drink a little more pleasant that it might otherwise be.

Note: because of the length of the 6th hole and the presence of the water at green-side, Fair Par allows Level 1 players four shots here to encourage them to be cautious and play the hole strategically. It is better, after all, to be a little short or a little left of this green with an iron you can trust, than to fly one into the pond because you put your faith in a wood or long iron that turned out to have a mind of its own.

Triggs Memorial Golf Course

1533 Chalkstone Avenue, Providence – 521-8460 – 18 holes

Scratch Par – 72
Fair Par Level 1 – 82
Fair Par Level 2 – 97

The adage that beauty is sometimes only skin deep applies to golf courses as well as to people. And while there might be public courses in the state that are more lush or better manicured than Triggs, there are few, if any, whose golf character is stronger.

It helped, of course, that Triggs got the best of starts in life, having been designed by Donald Ross in 1930, one of only two public courses in the state (Winnapaug is the other) to have benefited from the hand of the legendary Ross.

Over the years, Triggs has become something of an institution in Providence, as well as a green refuge in the busy city that has grown up around it. As a golf course, it is both a pleasure and a test. From the blue tees, in fact, the slope rating of 129 is among the highest in the state.

From the white tees the course plays only slightly shorter than from the blues, 6,302 yards to 6,522. The distance often means less than the wind, which seems always to be a factor here, because the course is situated on the one highest points of land in the city.

It doesn't take long for the challenge of the course to present itself, as the 2nd and 3rd holes are, respectively, the second and first highest-rated handicap holes on the front side.

At 445 yards long and a Scratch Par-4, #3 is particularly deserving of respect, for, in addition to the distance that must be negotiated, the travel must be accomplished over a rugged fairway that rises and dips and slopes throughout its length, presenting not only a nearly blind tee shot, but, potentially, a blind second shot.

The 437-yard 6th, is shorter than #3, but is rated a Scratch Par-5, principally because only big hitters are likely to get a clean look at the green on the second shot. The final quarter of the fairway doglegs hard to the right through a dramatic gateway of trees and bunkers to a downhill green.

One of the trickiest holes on the course is also one of the shortest: #7, a 185-yard test that plays uphill to a green that is fronted by a large, hungry bunker. The green itself is a slick maze of slopes that makes the difficult act of getting on in one shot no guarantee of finally making three on the hole.

The back side starts with two holes requiring approaches to uphill greens, and things get rugged again on the 13th, a 447-yard trial with a very hilly fairway and a load of fairway bunkers.

Players get a brief respite from long-distance travel at the 14th, a tidy downhill 140-yarder, with a raised green surrounded by bunkers, but things get long and large again at the rolling, 496-yard 15th.

If there is one hole that seems out of character at Triggs, it is #16, 302 yards long, with a very sharp, left-hand dogleg at the end. While most of the rest of the course has a rough and tumble challenge to it that includes a variety of ways to attack individual holes, this hole has a more plodding character that limits the ways golfer can approach it.

The course quickly returns to form, however, with what some players argue is the toughest pair of finishing holes in the state. Both the 17th, at 401 yards, and the 18th, at 399 yards, play into the prevailing breeze in the summer, and if, by this point, your golfing gas tank is starting to get low, this pair can rapidly use up the rest of your fuel.

Washington Village Golf Course

2 Fairway Drive, Coventry – 823-0010 – 9 holes

Scratch Par for 18 holes – 66
Fair Par Level 1 – 72
Fair Par Level 2 – 84

This 9-hole track, just off Route 117, is named for the tiny village of Washington. The course has had a topsy-turvy history, having gone through several changes of ownership and having been reconfigured from its original layout to fit plans for the housing development that now surrounds it.

In its current incarnation, the golf course plays to a Scratch Par of 66 for 18 holes and measures only 5,050 yards from the blue tees. Given that relatively short length, Fair Par at both Level 1 and Level 2 is rated from the blue tees, which adds about 200 yards or so to the overall distance for 18 holes.

Don't let the lack of distance fool you, however, for Washington Village is hardly a course that will let you get away without a fight. In fact, the strength of the golf course lies in its four shortest holes – the 1st, 3rd, 6th, and 8th – all of which are listed as Par-3s on the Scratch scorecard.

The opening hole, measuring 175 yards, plays over a wild area of vegetation, which can be visually distracting, to a green that stands a bit uphill from the tee. Even having to play over the miniature wilderness, the tee shot might not be a particularly complicated one were it not for a tall tree that stands along the right side of the fairway and that can easily catch a shot pushed in that direction.

The result is that players are faced with a difficult fact: very first swing of the day is a crucial one.

The 3rd hole, at 150 yards, is the shortest on the course, but it can be a trying one for players whose nerves get the better of them on the tee, for the majority of the distance to the green is covered by a pond that runs from the tee to the base of the sloping rise on which the green is built. Being short, therefore, is not a viable option, but because of the slope of the green and the rise it stands on, playing long can be dicey also, for there is little comfort in having to pitch back downhill toward

76

the green, and the pond below.

The 6th, 200 yards long, plays along a line of dense woods that edge more and more into play the closer you get to the green. Also lying close to play on both the right and behind the green are some very large boulders, placed there to create a border between the hole and the nearby residences.

The combination of the length of the hole and the trouble that lies on both the right and left makes #6 a Fair Par-4 for Level 1 players. The extra stroke is intended to encourage players to recognize the dangers of spraying a wood here in an attempt to snug the ball tight to the pin.

With the cushion of the extra shot, players can relax and realize they don't have to hit a home run, but can play a club they can control and that will get them to the vicinity of the front of the green, safely.

The 8th hole, at 200 yards, is just about the same length as #6, but Level 1 players are not allowed the extra shot here as they are at the 6th. Why? Because there isn't the same potential for disaster around the green as there is at #6, and players should feel a little freer to hit what they think it will take to get them onto the green.

In the end, if you have played these four short holes well, you have probably scored well overall. If not, at least you have fresh respect for the concept that distance isn't everything.

Weekapaug Golf Club

265 Shore Road, Westerly – 322-7870 – 9 holes

Scratch Par for 18 holes – 72
Fair Par Level 1 – 81
Fair Par Level 2 – 96

For most of its life, Weekapaug was known as Pond View, the name its builder and long-time owner, Sam Urso, gave it in honor of Winnapaug Pond, which borders the 3rd and 4th holes and which gives the course much of its character.

The 9-hole track was designed by Phil Wogan and opened to the public in 1967 – and, for a while, it seemed a perfectly good use of the land.

As time went on, however, the state's highways improved, access to South County from both upstate and out of state got easier, and this area, which had previously had seemed out of the way, became a magnet for tourists.

The more they visited, the more they wanted to live here, and by the 1980s, a full-scale land rush was underway. The value of property, particularly of land near the coast, skyrocketed, and developers, with visions of condos and dollar signs in their eyes, began to covet places like Pond View.

In the end, a group of local residents saved the day, as they managed to raise enough capital to acquire the golf course, clubhouse, and equipment, and to give the business a new lease on life as Weekapaug.

As far as the golf course itself goes, not much changed – and there's nothing wrong that, for the layout had always been a strong and underrated one. At 6,302 yards for 18 holes from the white tees and 6,440 yards from the blues, there's enough length to make things interesting. The holes vary nicely in look and approach from one to another, the ocean breezes present an ever-changeable challenge, and there are lovely views of the pond from a number of places on the course.

One other plus is that the club encourages players going around the nine twice to play the front nine from the white tees and the back from the blue tees.

That set-up doesn't affect the Fair Par rating at Level 2, which is 48 for each nine. It does change Level 1, however, by a stroke.

The difference comes at the 3rd hole, which, on average measures around 180 yards, and is bordered along the right side by the pond. It is a difficult hole because it plays into the prevailing summer breeze, and the approach is complicated by the pond and by a substantial bunker that lies just short and a little left of the green.

The difficulty of the hole can increase, at least psychologically, when the tee markers are placed on the right hand side of the teeing area, which forces players to hit more directly over the water, and raises the chance that they will end up in the drink.

On Weekapaug's official scorecard, the white tee for #3 is listed at 176 yards and the blue at 185, although that can change on any given day, depending on where the superintendent places the markers. Nevertheless, Level 1 golfers playing 18 holes at Weekapaug deserve an extra shot at least one of the two times they encounter #3, so the Level 1 Fair Par card sets Par from the blue tees at 4 and the white tees at 3.

Players should use the extra shot as a buffer against feeling they have to pull something out their bags that they are not going to be able to control. Remember, you are far better off ending up a little short on #3, even if it means being in the front bunker, than ending up at the bottom of the pond.

West Warwick Country Club

335 Wakefield Street, West Warwick – 821-9789 – 9 holes

Scratch Par for 18 holes – 70 men, 72 women
Fair Par Level 1 – 78
Fair Par Level 2 – 94

It is not clear why, but it seems that the history of some of the 9-hole golf courses in the state has been more turbulent than that of the 18-hole tracks. Perhaps, that's because a 9-hole course has less land associated with it and therefore is more readily bought or sold. Or, maybe 18-holes simply makes a golf course more of an institution, with more of the inertia of stability.

Whatever the reason, West Warwick is one of those 9-hole courses that, in its recent past has seen a change in ownership, one that converted the course from a strictly private club, to a public-access course that retains members and allows the latter preferred tee times and other privileges.

West Warwick is one of those courses that demands that golfers be ready to play before they step to the first tee, for it features one of the toughest opening holes you'll find anywhere: a 419-yard test that is rated as a Scratch Par-4. On the forgiving side, the hole is wide open. On the demanding side, however, the fairway has a decided right-hand slope to it, and side-hill lies on the second shot are not uncommon. The green is fronted by a large bunker, and it is also bunkered behind.

With good reason, the 1st is rated as the number-one handicap hole on the course. The optimistic way to view it is that, from here on in, things will get easier.

In some ways, the 2nd hole couldn't be more different from the 1st. With the latter, all the impending difficulties are visible from the tee. The 2nd is much more of a puzzle that can leave you wondering on the tee what the best strategy might be.

The tee is elevated well above the fairway, making the hole's 338 yards seem even shorter. But dense woods close in from both the left and the right, and, in the distance, a pond appears on the left side, lying short of the well-bunkered green.

If you're playing here for the first time, and you've got some pop in your driver, the temptation can be strong to try to whack the tee shot past the water – a risky proposition to be sure. But even if you decide on a lay-up, it can be difficult to estimate just how far you can hit to be safe. The best advice is to play the hole a few times and see for yourself.

The 3rd is an interesting Scratch Par-3 that plays uphill to a green surrounded by bunkers, including one directly in front that blocks a player's view of the green from the tee. The 4th continues the uphill trend, but this one is a wide open trek that features a rugged fairway, and that plays much longer than its 375 yards.

Players must then cross a street to reach the 5th hole, where the character of the course changes dramatically, going from the rugged, up and down terrain of the first four holes, to a much tamer, flatter, more park-like atmosphere that lasts through next three holes.

A note on Fair Par Level 1: holes 5-7 present no unusual difficulty, and each is rated at Par-4 on the Scratch card. But taken collectively and in the context of the entire nine, their difficulty exceeds 12 shots for a Level 1 player. Therefore, the Level 1 card allows an extra shot on #6, making it a Par 5.

The course finishes with two solid holes. The 8th measures 162 yards over a brook and a marshy area to a built-up green that falls away at its left, right, and back edges, and sports a bunker at the front right.

The 9th is 509 yards long, traveling over a fairly wide fairway that is marked by a tall, leafy tree that stands 150 yards or so in front of the tee. Anyone hoping to run up an approach to the green will find his ball caught by a wide bunker that lies just short of the green and across its entire front.

Winnapaug Country Club

Shore Road, Westerly – 596-1237 – 18 holes

Scratch Par – 72 men, 73 women
Fair Par Level 1 – 80
Fair Par Level 2 – 92

Winnapaug is one of two public golf courses in the state (Triggs is the other) to have had the benefit of design by golf architect Donald Ross, who remodeled the original nine holes here in 1921 and added nine more in 1928.

There are a number of memorable things about the golf course, but perhaps the most dramatic has nothing to do with golf, although it carries the same signature status as any golf hole might.

It is the huge, free-standing boulder that rises like a solitary monument along the left side of the 18th fairway, a remnant of times prehistoric, when Ice Age glaciers ground slowly but inexorably through the region, gouging out giant rocks, rolling them about as if they were pebbles, then leaving them wherever they lay as the weather finally warmed and the ice melted.

The course itself has several faces, offering a wide variety of holes, some of them very strong. The opener, for example, is (thankfully) benign, relatively short at 319 yards, and fairly trouble-free. It is followed by a rather rugged 480-yard test over a fairway that rises, falls, and slopes to the right toward a dense stand of woods.

The 3rd is a fine, 156-yard journey from an elevated tee, over a valley, to a green that is loaded with tricky slopes. And the 4th is a somewhat lengthy dogleg right, with a pond and trees at the right-hand corner, and a line of bushes and trees crowding in from the left – the number-one rated handicap hole on the front side.

One of the best holes on the course is the 9th, a 480-yard, downhill travel that bends steadily to the right. It is a hole that invites a player who can hit a long, straight drive and a solid second shot to make four. But there are dense woods to the left and more of the same to the right, posing plenty of trouble for players whose ambition exceeds their ability.

Beginning at #10, the course changes briefly but significantly, as golfers cross Shore Road to find four holes that give up the woodlands character of the other 14 holes in favor of a distinct seaside flavor. Tall trees give way to the grasses and shrubs typical of local salt marshes. The wind picks up, carrying the smells of the ocean. And the fairways get a lot flatter and a little less green. We are, after all, on the ocean side of the track.

The best hole of the group in this seaside pocket is the 12th. At 141 yards, it is the second shortest hole on the course, but the prevailing breeze tends to rush toward the tee. The green backs up hard to a salt pond, and there is a tendency to hit the ball shorter than one ought to, out of fear of the water behind. But that's better than the occasional overstrike, which spells disaster.

Players soon cross back over the road to re-enter the woods, and a number of good holes follow. The best of them, perhaps, is the 16th. At 150 yards from an elevated tee, across a valley, it is the parallel companion of the 3rd, except playing in the opposite direction, and it is a small gem.

The 17th is a sound hole as well, but its more important function is to bring players to the 18th tee and a good view of the signature Ice Age monolith, a sort of geological orphan, stranded beside the 18th fairway, predating not only the course but the invention of golf itself, witness to all manner of birdies and bogies, good swings and bad swings, the hopeful and the helpless. Local knowledge has it that a player could do worse than to hook a tee shot off the rock and send the ball pinging toward the green.

Woodland Greens Golf Club

655 Old Baptist Road, North Kingstown – 294-2872 – 9 holes

Scratch Par for 18 holes – 70 men, 72 women
Fair Par Level 1 – 78
Fair Par Level 2 – 92

Woodland Greens is the backyard playground for the residents of a condominium complex that surrounds this 9-hole course.

It is a tidy track that offers a variety of solid holes that range in difficulty from fairly easy to downright tough, and many holes sport large bunkers that rise up and intrude into the fairway from the rough.

For the purposes of variety, the Fair Par ratings here consider that golfers playing 18 holes will play from the white tees on the front nine and from the blue tees on the back nine.

The difference is only around 300 yards over 18 holes, and Fair Par at Level 2 is the same, 46, for each nine. Fair Par at Level 1, however, changes by two strokes, thanks to the 3rd and 8th holes. Both of those holes are rated as Scratch Par-3s, and from the white tees, they stand on the fringe of deserving an extra shot each at Level 1. When bumped back to the blues tees, the extra shots are added.

On #3, for example, the white tees measure 198 yards, and the hole plays over a valley that rises back up to the green. Bunkers lie to the front, left, and right of the green. Set up this way, it is a tough hole, but not necessarily one that might force a player to do something silly off the tee.

But the blue tees add 14 yards, and maybe even more than that psychologically. The result is that players now might be inclined to hit more club than they should, particularly an unpredictable wood, and end up spraying the ball into trouble.

The same is true on #8, but to a greater extent, for there is more trouble here. The hole measures 203 yards from the white tees and 225 from the blue. Green-side bunkers lie on both the left and right, but the biggest potential disaster is a steep slope at the back left of the green that leads to nothing but trouble.

From the blue tees, the natural tendency is to want to hit a club –

a driver or 3-wood for many players – that will cover the whole distance. The potential reward is being on the green in one shot and being able to putt for birdie. The risk is that you could just as easily – perhaps, far more easily – end up in the trees and worse, figuring out what it's going to take to avoid making five or six.

The extra shot for Level 1 players at both #3 and #8 is intended to replace anxiety with comfort on the tee, and to keep clubs that can lead to disaster in the player's bag, not in his hand.

In addition to these two holes, there are several other strong holes on the course. The 4th, for example, ranges from 505-525 yards, and doglegs left well out in the fairway. The corner is more than 200 yards from the tee and is both bunkered and treed. From there, the fairway runs uphill and includes a large fairway bunker that can snag many a hopeful second shot. More bunkers lie to both the left and right of the green.

The number-one handicap hole is the 9th, a Scratch Par-4 that plays close to 440 yards from the blue tees. One of the course's characteristic fairway bunkers lies on the right, waiting to catch tee shots. And farther up, in range of only the very big boomers off the tee, lies a sneaky pond that slides into play, almost unseen, from the right-hand rough.

RHODE ISLAND PRIVATE COURSES

Agawam Hunt Club

15 Roger Williams Avenue, East Providence – 434-3254 – 18 holes

Scratch Par – 70 men, 72 women
Fair Par Level 1 – 79
Fair Par Level 2 – 93

Agawam Hunt Club was founded in 1897, a time when gentility and good manners were considered attributes in polite society, but you would never guess it by stepping onto the club's 1st tee, where the opening hole (one of a handful of Donald Ross's originals that have survived subsequent radical design changes) is anything but mannerly.

In fact, it is a wonder that the 1st at Agawam merits only the second-highest handicap rating on the front side (behind the straight, flat, 437-yard 6th), for it is a 400-yard test that runs entirely uphill, with the first 200 yards or so rising like a wall. The climb moderates after that, but many players don't reach that more benign territory until their second shots, because the initial rise proves too severe to overcome with just the tee shot.

Pity the poor player who must face that opening challenge having just stepped from his car, with barely a practice swing or two for a warm-up.

That the 2nd hole is a true beauty likely will do little to keep first-time visitors at Agawam from wondering just what they are in for. Like the opener, #2 plays over some very rugged terrain, as the tee and green are separated by a deep valley, and the sloping, multi-level green falls away steeply both in front and on the right.

Fortunately for those who might be nervous over what else is in store, the course levels off for the next couple of holes, before the slope returns a bit on the lovely 145-yard 5th.

Level ground prevails again for several more holes – but that proves little comfort on the 266-yard 7th, where the tee shot must be played through a narrow chute of trees, over the Ten Mile River, and toward a green whose access features a colony of bunkers. "It's a nightmare," says one member. "One day you end up making 3, the next day you make 7."

Another short but tricky hole is the 329-yard 9th, where the final third of the fairway runs straight uphill, and the front left side of the green is a steep cliff that bottoms out in a sand bunker.

The 13th, the top-rated handicap hole on the back side, climbs the same hill, but with the addition of a stream that cuts across the fairway around 240 yards from the tee, and a number of bunkers that guard the approach to a very narrow green.

As we've mentioned, Donald Ross's original layout has been substantially altered over the years, as several holes that once lay on the southwest side of Pawtucket Avenue were relocated so members didn't have to cross the increasingly busy road. Some of those changes have not aged well and have, themselves, been altered in recent years.

One of those changes saw #16 converted from a dull, weak Scratch Par-4 to its original and rightful status as testy 162-yard Scratch Par-3, in which an undulating green nestles amid mounds and bunkers.

Another important change occurred on #15, which has gone from a mongrel to a monster. Until 1998, it was an almost semi-circular left-hand dogleg, measuring 418-yards from the white tees. Not only did the hole hook sharply to the left after crossing the Ten Mile River, but then it bent leftward again, and it was not impossible for a big hitter to consider trying to drive the green with a high, hooking tee shot.

In its new life, the hole is still a left-hand dogleg, but we're talking about a much bigger dog, as the distance has grown to 541 yards from the white tees. A new green backs up to a pond in what used to be the middle of the 16th fairway. Needless to say, the hole not only commands more respect than it did before, but also it earns status as a Par-6 at Level 1 and a Par-7 at Level 2.

Where Agawam lacks a friendly "hello" at the opening hole, it finishes with a more gracious, but not entirely gentle, "farewell", as the 410-yard 18th runs down the same hill that the first hole climbs. And where your drive on #1 was probably nothing to remember, catching the slope just right on #18 can make you feel like a big hitter indeed.

Alpine Country Club

251 Pippin Orchard Road, Cranston – 944-9760 – 18 holes

Scratch Par – 72 men, 73 women
Fair Par Level 1 – 81
Fair Par Level 2 – 95

There is no place in Rhode Island whose elevation above sea level can be considered truly high. At its peak, after all, the state can claim only lowly Jerimoth Hill, which climbs a mere 812 feet. Alpine Country Club, therefore, can't really live up to its name in the literal sense, despite standing well above much of the state on its hill in western Cranston. But that hasn't stopped the club from installing small A-frame rest stations around the golf course, designed to resemble the houses and huts one finds in the true alpine environs of, say, the Swiss Alps.

The thinner air of high altitude wouldn't hurt here, as players would be happy with a little more carry in their shots at Alpine, where the course measures more than 6,400 yards from the white tees. On the front nine alone, there are 3 holes that measure more than 500 yards from the whites. Another, #5, plays nearly 440 yards at Scratch Par 4, and one Scratch Par-3, #6, measures 205 yards.

For all its length, however, the course opens as any humane track should, with a short, wide hole that allows players the chance to ease into their rounds without being severely challenged before they are fully warmed up. Not only does the 1st at Alpine measure a mere 304 yards at Scratch Par-4, it even runs downhill, and you can't ask for much more than that. The only potential trouble is a pond that lies on the left and short of the green. There are also bunkers to the right and left of the green, but they bear the characteristic typical of most of the bunkers the course: they are shallow.

Don't take that to mean that bunkers aren't a factor at Alpine, for they are numerous, and they appear not only around the greens, but also in places in the fairways where drives tend to land or where a run-up type of approach to a green might be directed. But many of them are so shallow and lack any lip to speak of that putting your way out to reach a nearby green is often a reasonable possibility.

Following the break players get on the opening hole, they quickly face a test on #2, the first of several strong holes on the front nine. It measures 510 yards and plays slightly uphill, over a left-sloping fairway that is bordered by dense lines of trees. The fairway narrows and fairway bunkers appear as you approach the green, which is well guarded by shallow bunkers.

The top-rated handicap hole on the front is #5, a 438-yard Scratch Par-4. It is a hole on which a big drive would be a big help, but that idea is complicated by fairway bunkers on the left and right that spring up in an area 225-250 yards from the white tees.

The 8th is a very good hole, a wide, 540-yard dogleg right, whose fairway also slopes to the right, and it is followed by another nice one, the 141-yard 9th, which plays uphill to an undulating green that is raised above the fairway and surrounded by bunkers.

The back nine is a bit shorter than the front, but it also includes a problem that isn't present on the front: water. Small ponds first appear on the 11th hole, and another, larger one shows up on the 394-yard 13th, intruding from the right, about 125 yards from the hole and running to within 35 yards or so of the front edge of the green.

On the 374-yard 16th, water becomes even more intrusive, butting in at a point around 225 yards from the tee and eating up the left-hand half of the fairway. The course dries up again for the final two holes, but distance returns in the place of water to test players, as the 17th plays 390 yards and the 18th finishes at 420 yards, with both holes rated as Scratch Par-4s.

As you might expect, Alpine's length demands allowances under the Fair Par system. That applies particularly to the Level 2 players in this case, who are granted 23 strokes over the Scratch Par-72, including Par-7 ratings for the three longest holes on the front nine.

Level 1 players, on the other hand, receive a nine-stroke allowance over Scratch at Alpine, slightly less than the distance might seem to require at first glance, but the balancing factor is Alpine's generally level fairways. If Alpine's length were combined with the rugged terrain of, say, Misquamicut or Metacomet, the Level 1 Par might be closer to 91 that the 81 it is.

Glocester Country Club

Putnam Pike (Route 44), Harmony – 949-3330 – 9 holes

Scratch Par for 18 holes – 70 men, 73 women
Fair Par Level 1 – 76
Fair Par Level 2 – 90

Glocester Country Club is a short but lovely track set on the shores of Waterman Reservoir and along both sides of Route 44, as six holes lie to the south of the road, and three to the north. Although there are only nine holes in all, a number of them are memorable. And while the course measures less than 2,700 yards from the white tees and just a shade over 2,800 from the blue, some of the shorter holes are the most interesting, as well as the most problematic.

Take the opener, for example. From the white tees it is only 325 yards long, but the distance hardly tells the story, for beginning around 200 yards off the tee, a big set of mounds appears in the center and right side of a direct line to the hole. Above and behind the mounds looms a stand of trees. Meanwhile, the fairway begins to slope distinctly to the left and toward the reservoir as it doglegs around the mounds, and it narrows to almost nothing at one point. The mounded terrain continues along the right side of the fairway all the way to the green, which is a plateau set against a backdrop of trees. Approach shots hit long or left will meet disaster, for the green-side falls away wickedly toward trees and the lake.

The result is a hole that rewards a patient, well-placed tee shot and a careful approach. On the other hand, the hole can murder anything more reckless. For those reasons, and because it is the opening hole, Fair Par rates it a Level 1 Par-5. The hope, of course, is that players will use the extra stroke to play intelligently and get off to a good start, as opposed to ignoring the hole's obvious pitfalls, and then falling into them.

The 2nd is the shortest hole on the course at 153 yards, but a beauty nonetheless. Playing from an elevated tee, golfers have a wonderful look at a green set amid trees that close in from the right and left. A stream tumbles along the right side of the green and then crosses directly in front, and bunkers lie behind the green, ready to collect shots hit too far.

By contrast, the next two holes stretch out to more substantial lengths – 477 yards for #3 and 345 yards for #4 – but they are less interesting, for they flatten out and require less strategy. They are not without at least one problem, however, and it is a shared one: a stream that cuts across both fairways. It poses less of a problem at #3, for it runs straight across the fairway, around 135 yards from the green, a position that really shouldn't be in play on a second shot if you've hit a decent tee shot to begin with.

On the 4th, however, the angle at which the stream crosses the fairway can be diabolical, particularly for players who fade the ball. The problem is that the water intrudes on the left about 150 yards from the tee and then leaves the fairway at a point more than 200 yards out on the right, meaning that a fading drive that isn't hit all that well can begin to track the stream and drop into it almost anywhere along its length.

Players must cross Rt. 44 (or walk under it, through a tunnel) to reach the next three holes, the 401-yard 5th, a sharp dogleg right, and two shorter holes, #7 at 297 yards and #8 at 290 yards. What all three have in common are smallish greens that are raised above the fairway and fall away to one or more sides, which means they can be tough to hold, unless the approach shots land softly.

Back across the road lies the 8th hole, and the most treacherous tee shot on the course. The fairway is a rolling, sloping stretch that rises up in front of the tee and also falls away dangerously to the right, where dense woods wait to swallow errant drives. The green-side also falls away to the right toward a bunker and the trees beyond. Overall, the hole presents a good exercise in target golf, rewarding players who are willing to play to the safe spots in the fairway and penalizing those who just step up and whack drives recklessly from the tee.

The course finishes in lovely fashion, as the 158-yard 9th plays from an elevated tee, down to a green framed by trees, with the blue of the reservoir visible through the trees in the background.

Kirkbrae Country Club

Old River Road, Lincoln –333-1303 – 18 holes

Scratch Par – 71 men, 74 women
Far Par Level 1 – 81
Fair Par Level 2 – 94

Kirkbrae is elegant track that sprawls across a wide, mostly gentle hillside. The place was once a farm, and the clubhouse, until recent renovations, was based in a huge former barn. The golf course enjoys a decided park-lands setting that occasionally assumes a more woolly nature in places where the terrain becomes steep and rugged. For much of the course, however, stately, mature, well-spaced trees give the place a thoroughly civilized look.

Another recurring characteristic of the course is evident at the greens, where the putting surfaces are generously large, while being only lightly guarded by typically shallow bunkers. The greens are almost always built up at the back, inviting several types of approach shots, but penalizing those that go too far.

The course opens in compassionate fashion, with a relatively forgiving hole that plays 337 yards downhill from the blue tees (which are the middle men's tees here). The tee shot has a wide, invitingly look to it – always a psychologically welcome way to view the first shot of your golfing day. Around 200 yards from the tee, trees that pinch in briefly from the left and the right can pose problems, but the fairway widens out again after that as you approach a very accessible green.

The 369-yard 2nd is one of several holes that will reward a player who can hit the ball with authority and accuracy off the tee. The fairway rises and then dives hard toward the green, but about halfway out, it also slopes toward the trees on the left. Players who can keep the ball to the right (but out of the trees) and in the air for 175 yards or so will be able to catch the down-slope and make big progress toward the green. But players who let the left hand slope take over the tee shot can be in trouble.

Of the remaining seven holes on the front nine, two play more than 420 yards and one plays over 500 yards, and each sports some sort of rise in the fairway, which can make the distance a little more signifi-

94

cant. It's the sort of thing that can make a player wish he had more chances to play holes like #4, the shortest on the course, at 129 yards, a pretty little travel that plays over a small valley to a green tucked among a number of tall trees.

The back nine is interesting because of its variety, for it features what might be the most trying hole on the course (#14), the prettiest hole (#15), and two of the shortest but most strategically entertaining holes, #10 and #16. This pair have equal measurements from the white tees, 306 yards, and they are nearly mirror images of each other, for the 10th is a sharp dogleg left and the 16th is a hard dogleg right. And each hole presents the golfer with a decision on the tee: What kind of drive should I hit?

A player who can hook the ball will enjoy #10, but flirting too closely to the corner can be dangerous, for it is well guarded by a hill, bunkers, and trees. More trees line the tight, right-hand side of the fairway. A bunker short of the green and a severe drop-off behind mean that whatever choice you make on the drive had better be a good one to avoid having to hit some kind of scrambling shot to the green.

Conversely, a player who can hit a controlled fade is the happiest at #16, as the left side of the bending fairway is banked by a hill that tends to send balls scooting down into the fairway, and a fade will complement that situation well. But if you fade it too much, there is tree and terrain trouble on the right. The green is an uphill shelf that falls away disastrously to the right, so, once again, the tee shot needs to be good enough to put you in position to hit a soft, safe shot to the green.

The 494-yard 14th is a sweeping, uphill, right-hand dogleg, a potentially brutal trek, especially if you don't make something of yourself off the tee, which isn't easy because of the dogleg and a line of trees that stand tightly on the right. After that, the hole seems to climb straight up to a green that is cut into the hillside above. Any approach is a blind one, because, from below, players can only see the top of the flag, not the putting surface itself. To make things worse, two of the toughest bunkers on the course are cut to the front left and right of the green. The reward for enduring #14 is the lovely 15th, which plays 159 yards from an elevated tec, past a pond on the right, to a green that tilts invitingly toward the player.

Lincoln Country Club

Dexter Rock Road, Lincoln – 334-2200 – 9 holes

Scratch Par for 18 holes – 70 men, 71 women
Fair Par Level 1 – 78
Fair Par Level 2 – 90

The drive to Lincoln Country Club tells you plenty about what's in store for you on the golf course, for Dexter Rock Road is a true backcountry trail, full of twists and turns, rises and descents. And that's what the golf course at Lincoln is all about: rugged, back-country terrain that can jump or dive or turn without much advance notice, taking your golf ball, and your golfing fortunes, with it.

You get the first taste of it on the opening hole, a 346-yarder that passes a pond, which lies just off the tee to the right, and then bends a little left as it begins a gentle climb toward the green in an area 230 yards or so off the tee. At the same time, the fairway starts to roll and slope to the right, and there is ever less level fairway the closer you get to the green, which is a shelf cut into the hillside, with a steep fall-off to the right. The 345-yard 2nd hole plays back down the hill, but from an elevated tee that stands well above the 1st green. That increase in height makes for a beautiful look down at the right-bending fairway, which leads to a well-bunkered green.

Although the first two holes are about the same length, the 1st is rated a Level 1 Par-5, partly because it is the opening hole and partly because of the problematic uphill approach. The 2nd, on the other hand, is all downhill, and, with a hole under their collective belts, Level 1 players can't expect any allowance above the Scratch Par-4.

The 138-yard 3rd hole provides a gentle transition to an unusual and entertaining string of four holes, all of which have the same thing in common: a major rise in the fairway that blocks the view of the green from the tee and creates a blind tee shot on three of the holes.

Opening the stretch is the 359-yard 4th, a solid hole that requires a blind tee shot and penalizes drives that are hit too far left onto a fairway that slopes leftward toward trees. Once you reach the top of the initial hill, the approach to the green is a pretty one that plays through a gateway of trees that crowd the fairway from the left and right around 100 yards from the green. The fairway itself dives into a valley in front of the hillside green, which is framed on three sides by trees and guarded in front and on the left by bunkers.

On #5, 314-yards long, the tee shot plays across a valley and up to a hill that rises like a great barrier – hardly a shot that inspires confidence on the tee. The good news is that the fairway levels out at the 150-yard marker, but you need to hit the drive more than 200 yards (uphill) to avoid a blind shot to the green, which lies well below you on the other side of the hill. The fact is you need to be in the vicinity of the 100-yard marker to have a good view of the green on your second shot. The green is only lightly bunkered, but the trouble lies in a steep drop off behind, and from the vantage at the top of the hill, it is not difficult to make the mistake of hitting your approach too far and into disaster.

At the 451-yard #6 hole, it is the second shot, not the drive, that is blind, but the tee shot is no picnic either, for the fairway not only climbs steeply but also slopes hard into a deep depression on the right. The place to be is on the higher, more level ground of the left side of the fairway, but there is precious little of that, and it is tightly bordered by trees and out-of-bounds. When you finally reach the top of the hill, some 150 yards from the green, you find a potentially tricky approach before you to a green bordered on three sides by trees and bunkered well at the front left and right. The 6th is not the top-rated handicap hole on the course (#4 is), probably because it is relatively short for a Scratch Par-5, but the hole can play much longer than it's yardage indicates, and it is the only hole on the course that rates an extra stroke above Scratch at both Level 1 and Level 2.

The shortest of these middle four holes is the 7th, measuring 311 yards, but it presents the most trying tee shot of the group, for the drive must be played through a narrow line of trees, to a fairway that, in places, is absolutely side-hill, sloping hard toward the woods on the left. The reward here is that if you hit the ball straight off the tee, it stands a good chance of settling onto a flat area that lies on the left, near the woods at the bottom of the hill.

The prettiest hole by far on the course is the 8th, which plays from an elevated tee, along the face of the steep hill on the right, down to a green that, from the tee, appears to hover over a pond that abuts it on the left side and behind.

Louisquisset Golf Club

Overlook Circle, North Providence – 353-1620 – 9 holes

Scratch Par for 18 holes – 68
Fair Par Level 1 – 77
Fair Par Level 2 – 92

The tiny, crowded town of North Providence is known for a variety of things, but natural scenic beauty and tranquility are not among them. On the contrary, the commerical-strip nightmare of Mineral Spring Avenue is, for many a visitor, the impression that lingers. Yet, not far off that dizzyingly busy road – not much more than a Tiger Woods drive, in fact – lies the peaceful, 9-hole layout that is Louisquisset.

Once a full 18-hole track, Louisquisset was downsized a number of years ago to make room for a sprawling community of condominuims, whose clapboarded buildings now line, and often define, the remaining nine holes. In addition to cutting the size of the course in half and forcing a redesign of several holes, the condos had one other lasting effect: they were placed close enough to the golf course that the fairways are literally the backyards of many residents. Then, to reduce the impacts of golf on the daily lives of these residents – impacts that can involve the damaging effects of errant golf balls – out-of-bounds stakes were set everywhere along the edges of the holes. There might be more OB at Louisquisset, in fact, than at any golf course in Rhode Island. The result for golfers is a premium on accuracy, particularly on driving accuracy, on many parts of the course, along with the resulting substantial penalties for those who stray.

At a length of less than 2,700 yards even from the blue tees, the course is decidedly short, but it is no pushover. Golfers stepping to the first tee quickly realize that, as they face a nearly 400-yard test, in which the opening shot of the round must carry a good-sized pond that lies in front of the tee. Out-of-bounds stakes pinch in tightly from both the right and left in an area where many a player might try to land a drive, and from there the fairway climbs to a green that lies above them. In short, the hole can be both a difficult opener and an example of the several solid holes players encounter on the course.

The next good hole is #3, the only Scratch Par-5 on the course, playing around 450 yards down a gradual slope. The challenge here, as on the majority of holes at Louisquisset, is the tee shot, which must be played along a line of trees and fencing that runs tightly along the entire right side. That restriction, combined with the fact that the fairway eventually bends hard to the right, means that players who like to fade the ball have a distinct advantage, while players who tend to draw their tee shots can be in big trouble. Yet, even left-to-right players have to contend with the fact that the fairway bottlenecks severely between OB stakes and other obstacles in a prime landing area.

Turns out that two of the other potentially tough holes on the nine, #6 and #9, also favor the fader, for both holes bend to right, and players who can hit solid, accurate, left-to-right tee shots can put themselves in positions to profit.

One oddity of Louisquisett, perhaps a welcome one for many players, is that there is nary a fairway bunker on the golf course – and, in reality, the bunker that fronts the final green is probably the only sand of any kind at Louisquisset that presents a strategic challenge. With only two other exceptions, the remainder of the greens on the course are all but unguarded.

One of those exceptions is #5, a Scratch Par-3 measuring 172 from the white tees and 187 from the blues. The hole is complicated by two elements: a pair of large mounds at the front left and right of the green, and very tight OB behind the green. Because of those potential problems and that fact that Louisquisset encourages golfers going around twice to play the front nine from the white tees and the back nine from the blues, Fair Par at Level 1 rates the hole differently from the two tees.

From the whites, it is rated a Level 1 Par-3, but as the distance grows from the blue tees, players can be tempted to feel they have to bring large weapons to bear on the tee shot – weapons like woods. But a wood and a big swing are recipes for disaster here, which is why the hole is rated a Par-4 at Level 2. With that cushion, the idea is that players will be much better off aiming a middle iron they can trust toward the opening between the mounds at the front of the green, rather than risking spraying a longer iron or wood out of bounds or behind the mounds.

Metacomet Country Club

Veterans Memorial Parkway, East Providence – 434-9588 – 18 holes

Scratch Par – 70 men, 72 women
Fair Par Level 1 – 80
Fair Par Level 2 – 95

A 1901 Donald Ross design, the course at Metacomet features as much rugged up and down terrain as you'll find in the state, and as much variety from hole to hole. In fact, it would be difficult to find more than a hole or two on this course that doesn't have something interesting, entertaining, or unusual about it.

That uniqueness even extends to the scorecard, which lists only two sets of yardage for each hole, "Championship" and "Ladies," despite the fact that each teeing area has a set of white tee markers, in addition to the blue and red markers. Official distances for the white tees are available only on the Scratch Par-3 holes, where granite ground markers, imbedded in the tees, list both the championship yardage and the middle distance. On the other holes, the Fair Par scorecards assume that the white markers stand an average of 10 yards short of the championship tees and they list the middle yardage that way.

The entertainment at Metacomet starts on the opening hole, which plays 376 yards over a rise and then down a slope to the green. It's not a difficult beginning if you hit the tee shot well and catch the slope, but straying can be a problem. For that reason, and because it is the first hole, players at both Fair Par Level 1 and Level 2 are granted extra shots here.

The 2nd is a 462-yard, sharp right-hand dogleg around a brackish cove – a relatively easy Scratch Par-5, providing you can stay out of the water. The respite is brief, however, as the uphill, 349-yard 3rd provides not only a good-looking hole, but also an early test of shot-making. The intimidating tee shot must be made over a marsh to a fairway that bends right, slopes right, climbs uphill, and is bordered tightly by large trees. The approach is even more interesting, for it is to a slick, shelf green that is cut into the hillside above. Bunkers are cut into the green-side face on the left and right, and another deep bunker lies to the right of the green.

The 4th is a 446-yard dogleg right, that plays from an elevated tee, deep into a lowland, and then back up to a treacherous hillside green. The hilly adventure continues at the 168-yard 5th, which plays uphill to another shelf green, whose green-sides fall away sharply, left into trees, right into steep disaster. More rugged terrain rises in front of the tee on the 441-yard 6th, as the fairway climbs before you like a tidal wave, then plateaus awhile before diving into a small valley. The 7th is friendlier but still part of the roller coaster, playing 145 yards from an elevated tee, through tall trees, down to a green well guarded by round-mounded, deep bunkers.

The 453-yard 9th is almost completely flat and straight for most of its length, but as you move within short iron distance of the green, the fairway grows ever skinnier. It also begins falling away along its edges, until, finally, all that's left that isn't hillside is the green itself, which has the look of the bow of a ship raised up above a sea of green.

The back nine features two very challenging Scratch Par-3 holes — #10 and #12 — but the former is the most dramatic. Facing 208 yards from the middle marker, players have virtually no good place to land the tee shot except on the green. The tee is elevated above a deep valley, and the terrain doesn't become level again until it meets the front edge of the green. You don't even want to *think* about being short. The same advice applies to being left, because the terrain falls away fatally on that side of the green. Things aren't quite so bad behind or to the right of the green, but they aren't good, especially because being in either place means having to play back in the direction of the abyss

The remainder of the nine features much of the same rolling thunder terrain as the front, and, as you might expect, the course finishes in that fashion. The 392-yard 17th is a sweeping left-hand dogleg that plays from an elevated tee to a wide valley and back uphill to the green. The 337-yard 18th also plays from a height into a wide valley, and then to a lovely, built-up green that is guarded by several big bunkers, artistically scalloped into the green-sides.

The Misquamicut Club

Ocean View Highway, Watch Hill – 348-8121 – 18 holes

Scratch Par – 69 men, 71 women
Fair Par Level 1 – 81
Fair Par Level 2 – 91

When a golf hole is praised as having "character," the suggestion is that the hole is distinguished by elements that make it something other than a flat, green trail leading, without adventure, from the tee to the hole. Holes with character are those that, through a combination of lay-out and good looks, stand out in your mind after a round, and even a good course is lucky to boast more than a handful holes that fit that description.

At The Misquamicut Club, however, there are so many holes that have something truly different, interesting, beautiful, or memorable about them that you would save time trying to count the ones that don't.

Established in 1895 and designed by Donald Ross, the course is hardly long, measuring less than 5,800 yards from the white tees and just over 6,200 from the blues. Nor is it marked by a large population of bunkers the way some of the state's other premier courses are. What the course has, instead, is terrain – wild, rolling, leaping, diving, terrifying, exhilarating terrain.

Through the first 11 holes, for example, there is only one, #5, on which the progress from the tee to the green might not induce some form of vertigo or seasickness in those who might be a tad weak in the stomach, for it seems that every shot in that stretch is played either to or from a significant piece of elevation, or across some piece of fairway that boils with undulation.

Even when the course finally flattens out on holes 12-17, other elements – wind and water – appear, for at that point the course has turned to face the Atlantic Ocean, and one hole after another plays either over or around the ponds and marshes that lie in the lowlands behind the sand dunes of the adjacent beach.

The uninitiated can be excused for not knowing what they're in for at first, as the driveway into the club brings you to the elegant, turn-of-the-century clubhouse and the tranquil green lawn that spreads before it – a setting that speaks of calm and comfort. But things change quickly, for the walkway leading behind the clubhouse brings you to the first tee and an intimidating view of the first hole – a 379-yard affair, with a fairway that rolls and tumbles like a stormy sea.

About halfway down the 395-yard 2nd hole, the fairway drops precipitously, rewarding a big hitter who can get to the bottom on a drive, but leaving shorter hitters with problems. The challenge continues at the 221-yard 3rd hole, a brutal Scratch Par-3 played over a decidedly uneven fairway. Golfers hoping for a break at the 257-yard 4th find themselves faced with a rollicking fairway that rises to a green that is staunchly guarded by bunkers.

The green at the185-yard 6th is edged by a cliff that falls away to a place where you simply do not want to be, and the 8th plays 155 yards to a green that is set atop what looks like a small extinct volcano, whose peak was blown off long ago, leaving a plateau putting surface in its place.

At the 353-yard 9th, the green stands above the rugged fairway on a shelf cut into the hillside. And the fairway at the 366-yard 10th might be the most radical of all, as it dives from the tee and then wraps around a giant mound that rises on the left side, creating something of a dogleg.

The course moves into its seaside mode at the 308-yard 11th, which plays grandly from an elevated tee toward the ocean. Next is perhaps the best hole on this part of the course, the short but dangerous 12th, which plays 127 yards from a tee set amid sand dunes, over a pond, to a green set below and behind the dike that holds the pond back.

The course returns to its rugged dry-land side for the finish, closing in dramatic fashion with the nasty but memorable 191-yard 18th, which plays over a valley and up to a green set at the crest of a steep hill. Anyone needing to score a three to win a match here will have his hands full.

Newport Country Club

Harrison Avenue, Newport – 846-0461 – 18 holes

Scratch Par – 72
Fair Par Level 1 – 83
Fair Par Level 2 – 96

Newport Country Club, with its rich history and wind-swept, seaside layout, is one of the best known golf clubs not only the state but in the entire Northeast. The club made a name for itself back in 1895, when it was the site of the first United States Amateur and Open Championship (the Amateur and Open being the same tournament in those days).

The golf club was founded in 1893 to provide summer recreation for the wealthy families whose grand "cottages" still stand today along Bellevue Avenue, Ocean Drive and at other high rent addresses in town. In 1915, facing changes in golf created by better equipment that made many course designs obsolete, Newport underwent extensive remodeling by architect Donald Ross. The results have held up well enough that in its recent history, the course has hosted PGA Senior Tour events, and, in 1995, the centennial of the United States Amateur, won by Tiger Woods.

Newport is considered a links course, and as such it is characterized by a near absence of trees, although there are plenty of low, thick bushes that can swallow golf balls as quickly as any wooded area. Like links courses, there is almost always wind here, most of it coming from Rhode Island Sound, which almost abuts the course to the south.

And there is sand, lots and lots of it in the ubiquitous bunkers that fill the fairways and surround the greens. The fact is that if your sand wedge isn't working, a round at Newport can be a trial, and although the golf course is not especially long, measuring 6,111 from the white tees, the sheer number and placement of the bunkers can make it seem much longer. There are few tee shots, for example, that can be struck without considering the whereabouts of one or more fairway bunkers, and the same is true of second shots on the longer holes. And there are almost no approach shots that can be made without considering the bunkers that threaten to snatch not only balls but golfers' hopes for a good score.

The character of the course shows itself on the first hole, a Scratch Par-5 on the scorecard that measures only 442 yards. But on most summer days the hole plays longer than that because the prevailing wind blows almost directly at the tee. Bunkers that can catch tee shots lie to both sides of the fairway. And even if you have managed to negotiate a good tee shot, your task is far from over, for the approach is to a raised green that is heavily bunkered on all sides.

Neither of the next two holes is long either, but both play into the sea breezes, and #4, at 181 yards, runs parallel to the coast, where the wind can shove tee shots into any one of several bunkers.

The first assist players get from the summer breeze is on #5, but the relief is short lived, for the fairway is fraught with bunkers, particularly on the left side, but also on the right. At 411 yards, the 5th is rated the number-one handicap hole on the front side.

One of the best holes on the front side is the 7th, which measures 493 yards and features a vast field of bunkers along the left side of the fairway that rise toward players like lines of breaking ocean waves.

Among the most memorable pieces of the golf course are the pair of Scratch Par 3 holes, the 13th and 14th, which lie on either side of the clubhouse. The former measures only 137 from the white tees, but that's the only easy element of the hole, for the tee shot is not only into the wind, but uphill to a shelf of a green that is surrounded by some of the most treacherous green-side bunkers on the golf course.

Then comes #14, whose tee stands almost on the clubhouse patio, commanding a lovely view to the south of the golf course and the ocean beyond. It also offers a stark view of what lies immediately in store for golfers: a 200 yard hole that not only plays into the wind, but portends disaster for anyone who happens to pull a tee shot to the left, where both the fairway and the green-side fall away steeply, leading players into nothing but trouble.

Pawtucket Country Club

900 Armistice Boulevard, Pawtucket – 726-6320 – 18 holes

Scratch Par – 69 men, 73 women
Fair Par Level 1 – 79
Fair Par Level 2 – 94

Founded in 1901, the Pawtucket Country Club offers golfers the graceful setting of a mature, cultivated park, with stately trees throughout and little or no undergrowth. The terrain is relatively flat and there are few fairway bunkers, a combination that gives the holes a wide open look – something that, of course, can prove an illusion depending where the rough starts.

The clubhouse and the 1st tee are set a stone's throw from the Ten Mile River, and the river is visible through the trees on several holes along the front nine, but aside from a small pond set directly in front of the 1st tee, there is no water in play anywhere on the course.

The course begins with a hole that qualifies as a tough opener. If you're not particularly warmed up on the first tee, the hole's 380-yard length will seem substantial. And it includes a psychological hurdle, for the fairway rises a bit before you, and from the tee, the impression is that this one will not be an easy driving hole.

The 2nd isn't easy either. At 407 yards, it is a good-looking, solid test featuring a fairway that, at about 230 yards off the tee, starts rolling and then takes a quick dive into a valley along the left side.

An oddity follows: back to back, side by side holes that have the same yardage from the white tees. The 3rd and 4th abut one another, although they run in opposite directions, and each is listed on the scorecard as measuring 369 yards. Each carries a Scratch Par-4 rating and a Fair Par Level 2 rating of Par 5.

The difference occurs at Fair Par Level 1, where the 3rd is rated at Par-5 and the 4th at Par-4. The reason has everything to do with terrain: #3 plays uphill and offers a less than reassuring view from the tee, while #4 runs downhill, offering players not only a more encouraging aspect from the tee, but a better look at the green from the fairway.

An interesting hole on the front side is the 161-yard 7th, which

106

doesn't look like much from the tee, but things get complicated around the green, thanks to a deep bunker that runs entirely across the front of the green, green-side bunkers left and right, and a substantial fall-off behind.

The front nine finishes with that side's top-rated handicap hole, a 436-yard travel to a green that backs up to a stand of pines. Players hitting approaches to the green should be cautioned that being long is a bad idea, because the green-side falls away hard in the back, and having to play a third shot from there is far less preferable than playing from almost anywhere short of the green.

The back nine features four Scratch Par-4 holes over 400 yards long, each of which is rated at Fair Par-5 at Level 1 and at Par-6 at Level 2. The longest is the 12th, which at 433 yards is the top-rated handicap hole on the back side. Not only is it long, but the green can be a difficult platform, for it is built up enough that it falls away steeply at the left and behind, and the putting surface itself has several levels to it.

Players might find that their favorite hole on the back nine is the final one, a wide beauty that plays 365 yards, with about half of that distance running decidedly downhill. In fact, players who can fly the tee shot 180 yards or so will be rewarded with a big bounce and roll, as the ball will strike the fairway on its down slope.

That also is the area where the hole gets especially handsome, as players get a good view of the green, which is set at the bottom of a kind of bowl cut out from the hill behind. The green is surrounded by bunkers, and above it, the large white clubhouse presides.

In all, the hole is a lovely example of golf course architecture – and it doesn't hurt that, with the help of a solid drive, the hole offers players the chance to finish on a positive note.

Point Judith Country Club

150 Windemere Road, Narragansett – 792-9770 – 18 holes

Scratch Par – 71 men, 72 women
Fair Par Level 1 – 81
Fair Par Level 2 – 94

The only golf course in Narragansett, Point Judith was built as a playground for the wealthy summer residents who, around the turn of the 20th century, constructed elegant summer houses in the neighborhood behind Narragansett town beach and along the rocky coast that fronts Ocean Road.

The original course consisted only of an old fashioned nine holes. Then, in 1927, the club hired architect Donald Ross to bring the original nine up to "modern" standards, and add nine more. In 1996-97, the course got yet another makeover, as members sought to add some character and difficulty to the front nine, as well as places for surface water to drain, The result was a bunch of new bunkers and ponds that provide both hazards and good looks to the first several holes.

Among the holes that needed the least character-rebuilding are some of the shortest on the course – beginning with the shortest of all, #9, which measures only 120 yards from the white tees, but plays to one of the tiniest greens you'll find anywhere. Not only that, but this postage stamp is virtually imprisoned by bunkers, which lie to the front, left, and right. The good news is that a golfer who manages to land a ball on the green stands a very good chance of making birdie, because the green is so small there is no such thing as a long putt. The bad news is that it is far easier to hit a tee shot into one of the green-side bunkers than onto the green, and the size of the green leaves little room for mistakes when playing out of those bunkers.

The next short hole of interest is the 14th, which, at 326 yards, is a deceptive little test in that it doesn't look like much from the tee. Dense woods crowd in from the left, and there are also trees to the right, but even so, the tee shot isn't the problem.

More treacherous by far is the second shot. First, the green, which lies above the fairway, is fronted by a huge bunker, so the natural ten-

108

dency is to want to hit the approach shot hard enough to make sure you can carry the bunker. But it turns out that the raised-up green falls away steeply on the left, right, and back, and balls hit long can end up in the trees.

The 15th hole, measuring 357 yards, also is not long, but it offers some of the same trouble as the 14th, including the built-up green, backed by woods, which penalizes players who hit the ball too far on the approach. The hole is also complicated by a left-sloping fairway that can kick balls toward the woods on the left, and by a hidden pond on the right, that hides out of sight in a depression behind weeds and brush around 120 yards from the green.

Another very good, but short hole follows at #16, which plays 196 yards over a pond to a well-bunkered green. As fraught with potential disaster as this hole is, it does not warrant being ranked as a Par-4 at Fair Par Level 1, and there are two reasons. The first is that the hole tends to play downwind more often than not, making it shorter than the yardage would indicate.

Second, the biggest trouble here – the pond – lies short of the green, and giving Level 1 players an extra stroke on a Scratch Par 3 hole is usually aimed at encouraging them to hit a little less club than it would take to get them all the way to the hole. In this case, however, players are definitely better off being long and dry, rather than short and wet.

For similar reasons, the 204-yard 11th hole also remains a Par-3 at Level 1. In that case, most of the trouble comes in the form of two very large bunkers that lie short of the green, one on the right and the other on the left. Again, this is a hole on which players might as well play for the flagstick rather than the front of the green, since there is a greater potential penalty for being short than for being long.

Potowomut Golf Club

Ives Road, Warwick – 884-9773 – 18 holes

Scratch Par – 71 men, 73 women
Fair Par Level 1 – 81
Fair Par Level 2 – 93

Among the categories of golf course types, one is set aside for "park lands" courses, and Potowomut might be one of the courses in the state that best fits that description. The place is lush, genteel (though not always gentle), and resplendent with mature trees that were probably saplings when the club was established in 1927. At just over 6,000 yards from the white tees, a shade under 6,400 from the blues, and a Scratch Par of 71, Potowomut is hardly a long course, and, in fact, the shortest holes here, the collection of Par-3s, are among the most memorable.

That group of four holes begins with the 3rd, which plays 143 yards from an elevated tee to a small green that is completely surrounded by bunkers. It's not a long hole and there are no tricks to it – what you see is what you get – but members will tell you that it might produce more strokes over Par than any other hole on the course.

The next is the 179-yard 6th, which plays through a narrow chute of trees that tends to force tee shots to the left while the hole bends a little to the right. A fairway bunker can catch shots that fall short, and the narrow green is well-bunkered on both the left and the right.

The 12th is the longest of the Par-3s, playing 187 yards from the white tees to another well-bunkered green. And just to the right and little short of the green, an unseen pond lies in wait behind a fringe of weeds.

The best of the group is the shortest, #16. It plays 139 yards uphill to a shelf of a green that sits above a big bunker at the right front. The tee shot not only needs to be played high to carry to the top of the rise and then land softly, it must negotiate a narrow opening to the green framed by tall trees to either side.

From the point of view of Fair Par Level 1, this group of four holes presents a problem. Individually, none of them is long enough to warrant being rated a Par-4, but, taken collectively, it is unlikely that Level 1 players are going have an easy time playing the group in 12 shots. For that reason, the Level 1 rating has been liberal for several other holes that might otherwise be on the borderline of qualifying for extra shots – in particular, the 2nd, 4th, and 14th – so that the overall Level 1 Fair Par rating of 81 is equitable for the golf course from the white tees.

Despite the strength of Potowomut's short holes, the course is not without notable longer holes, and the best among them, perhaps, is also the longest, the elegant 15th. Measuring 507 yards, the hole sweeps grandly to the left through an alley of tall, spreading trees. A pair of large bunkers guards the right side of the fairway, and they can be a nemesis for players who might be inclined to fade the ball on their second shots. On the other hand, the hole can be a delight for players who can draw the ball consistently.

The back nine finishes with two good holes, including another that favors a hook, the 17th. At 371 yards, it plays from an elevated tee to a fairway that bends to the left around large, leafy trees. The hole also plays into the prevailing breeze in the summer, and that, combined with the left-hand attitude of the fairway, makes a fader's difficulties even more complicated. In the worst case, a slice from the tee can be carried by the wind all the way to the pond on the 18th hole.

Speaking of the finishing hole, it is a 367-yard dogleg that jogs sharply to the right over said pond. Trees grow along the right-hand side of the pond, preventing players from taking the shortcut to that side and forcing them to play their tees shots directly in front of the pond, which covers most of the last third of the fairway. To make things even more interesting, the green is raised above the fairway, meaning that the approach shot not only has to carry the water, it must travel uphill, and be high enough to land softly. The 18th is not a long hole, particularly because it tends to play downwind, but it can be the sort of hole that makes a player glad that the 19th hole is only a few steps from the green.

Quidnessett Country Club

950 N. Quidnessett Road, North Kingstown – 885-5613 – 18 holes

Scratch Par – 72
Fair Par Level 1 – 84
Fair Par Level 2 – 97

There might not be a golf course in the state that has a more dramatic dual personality than Quidnessett – personalities that trade places not gradually, nor even from one hole to another, but in the middle of the fairway of one particular hole.

It is a dichotomy that has roots in the way the course was developed, beginning in 1960 when the first 18 holes opened as a mostly inland course, with another nine holes planned that would make use of land lying along the shore of Narragansett Bay. But in the early 1970's, the club learned it would be unable to renew a lease it held on property that included a number of its holes. The club then had to switch strategies and redesign much of the existing course, as well add new holes to replace ones that were scheduled to disappear when the leased land was returned to its owner.

The result is a golf course that, for the first 10½ holes, has the wide open look of manicured pasture land, tastefully and strategically planted with a variety of trees, although not enough to create any sense of a dense woodland. And water of any significance appears in only one isolated place. On the 524-yard 11th hole, all that changes.

Players are offered a foreshadowing of what is to come on the 11th tee, for the blue of Narragansett Bay can be seen filling the background between the trunks of the trees in the distance, but the immediate fairway retains the wide open feel of its predecessors. Then, at a spot around 130 yards from the green, it becomes apparent why the hole is named "Hourglass," as trees and marshland suddenly pinch in hard from both the right and the left, reducing the fairway to only a handful of yards in width.

The constricted waist also forms a sort of gateway, as players journey into the course's second world, one that leads them through an amphitheater of trees before releasing them on the 14th hole to a Bay-side environment. This finishing section has a decided links look to it and includes some of the very best holes on a course where very good holes are the rule, not the exception.

That general level of excellence is evident early on the front nine, at the 505-yard 3rd hole. Appropriately, the hole is named "The Snake," for it follows a winding route, bending first left between trees and fair-way bunkers, then back to the right around a trio of bunkers that lie a short iron from the green. The green itself is set in a bit of a hollow and is wrapped, as most of the greens on the course are, in large bunkers.

The number-one handicap hole follows, a 450-yard, Scratch Par-4, which, for all its length can seem harmless compared to the next hole, which plays 168 yards, often into the wind, almost entirely over a pond.

Quidnessett's idea of an easy hole is the 9th, a 496-yard dogleg left, which offers a fairly wide driving area, as well as approach shots that often play downwind. The catch is that things tighten up consider-ably 50 yards or so in front of the green, where a giant bunker on the left and another bunker on the right close in on the fairway. The small green is also well-bunkered left and right. The hole is called "Birdie Lane," but don't get your hopes up

Perhaps the most memorable holes are found among the final five, which not only play along Narragansett Bay, but through, over, and around a tidal marsh thick with tall, graceful grasses. Wind is a major factor, as it tends to blow either at the backs or in the faces of the play-ers. Bunkers are everywhere, marching up fairways and surrounding greens. And the final hole, named "Perfect Ending," lives up to its name, playing 367 yards, into the prevailing breeze, between lines of marsh-land, and, finally, over the marsh to the green.

It is not an accident that Fair Par at both Level 1 and Level 2 is high – 84 and 97 respectively – for the golf course is a test, and at 6,500 yards from the white tees and 6,940 from the blues, is one of the longest tracks in the state.

Rhode Island Country Club

150 Nyatt Road, Barrington – 245-7370 – 18 holes

Scratch Par – 71 men , 74 women
Fair Par Level 1 – 82
Fair Par Level 2 – 97

Rhode Island Country Club is a Donald Ross design, loaded with Ross trademarks, particularly on the shorter holes, where the greens often have the look of oversized stumps, sitting several feet above the fairway, cloaked in green, and surrounded at the base by sand bunkers.

Overall, the golf course has a number of personalities that alternately offer holes with flat park-like settings, holes whose terrain is entirely rough and tumble, in-land holes with significant fresh-water hazards, and the four finishing holes that border Narragansett Bay, where the wind and the sweeping view of the water defines the character of the holes as much or more than their layout and topography do.

One thing that is not at all in short supply at RICC are bunkers, both of the fairway and green-side variety, and players are introduced to that aspect of the course right away, as the opening hole features a march of left-side fairway bunkers that begins within easy striking distance of the tee and continues all the way to the green. More bunkers sprout on the right just short of the green, and this abundance of sand, combined with the fact that it is the opening hole, wipes out any advantage that the hole's modest 359-yard length and the downhill travel might offer golfers. As a result, this Scratch Par-4 is the first hole on the course, but hardly last, to earn the allowance of an extra stroke at Level 1 to push it to a Par 5.

The 366-yard 2nd gives players an early indication of how tough some of the approach shots will be on this course, for the green's architecture is a type that quickly becomes familiar at RICC: a raised up shelf with steep sides that in places are merely grassed, but in others are scooped out and filled in with sand.

The 3rd provides a good lesson in what Ross was fond of doing with rugged terrain: instead of avoiding it and routing the course around it, he built holes directly over it. The result is a hole that is relatively short at 311 yards, but one that rises and falls enough to make finding a good place to hit a drive, and then a second shot, far from an easy task.

One of the most interesting holes on the front side is #8, a 438-yard Scratch Par-5. From the tee, the flat, open driving area offers the promise of a free ride to the green. Then, a little more than halfway to the hole, everything suddenly changes. The fairway drops quickly and unexpectedly, and then bottoms out into four side-by-side bunkers that spread across the fairway depression. Just past the bunkers, the fairway rises, then falls again, and a pond intrudes from the left. Once again, the fairway climbs to support a green that is tucked on the left side, behind the pond and against a line of trees.

Two of the most two memorable holes on the back side are the finishing pair, the picturesque, 120-yard 17th, the club's signature hole, and the gut-wrenching 332-yard 18th, whose approach to the green separates those who want to win a match from those whose nerves will desert them when they need them most. The former is the shortest hole on the golf course, but if the wind off the Bay is right, it will hardly seem short. And while you might be tempted under other circumstances to hit a lower trajectory, knock-down type of shot to minimize the effects of the wind, the green demands otherwise, for it is one of those lovely, built-up, round-shouldered affairs that falls off to bunkers around its entire perimeter.

The final hole offers relatively little trouble off the tee, but over the last third of its length, the hole plays uphill to a sloping, heavily bunkered green. The biggest, deepest bunker is cut into the hill below the green on the left side. Smaller bunkers lie to the right and behind the green, and although they might look benign, having to play from them to a green that lies not only below but slopes away will make you wish you'd practiced the shot before you had to play it. One other thing: a cart path and out-of- bounds lie immediately to the back left of the green. In other words, be prepared to drop a high, soft approach shot directly onto the green (or least to the front edge), or be prepared for problems.

Sakonnet Golf Club

79 Sakonnet Point Road, Sakonnet – 635-4706 – 18 holes

Scratch Par – 69 men, 70 women
Fair Par Level 1 – 77
Fair Par Level 2 – 92

Founded in 1899, Sakonnet was designed by Donald Ross, and the architect was also a member of the club – which makes it all the more intriguing that the course has a very different look from a number of other courses in the state that Ross had a hand in designing.

Where changes in elevation, contours of fairways, and placement of greens at other Ross courses, notably Metacomet and Misquamicut, are nothing short of tumultuous, those elements at Sakonnet are almost uniformly tame. Nor, in some of his other designs, was Ross shy about using trees to complicate things, but much of Sakonnet is virtually tree-less. Even when trees weren't available or practical at other Ross designs, such as Newport Country Club, he made up for it with lots of sand bunkers. But at Sakonnet, while bunkers can come into play, many of the greens are untroubled by them, and truly bothersome fairway bunkers are few.

Add to all that the fact that the course measures only 5891 yards, at Scratch Par-69, from the blue tees (the white markers are the forward-most here), and you have a course that offers a decidedly open, unobstructed, user-friendly experience.

The explanation is that Ross and his wife spent their summers in Sakonnet, and the otherwise demanding architect decided to build a course here that would be gentle on his spouse. One imagines that Ross also was protecting himself, in the knowledge that if he made the home course too severe, the lady of the house, after a day on the links, might be more inclined to be throwing pots and pans around the kitchen than cooking with them.

The result is that there are none of the hillside lies and awkward stances so common at, say, Misquamicut, nor any of the climbing and descending that players at Metacomet routinely endure. What there is at Sakonnet in abundance, however, is wind, for the course is situated hard by the eastern shore of Sakonnet River and not far at all from the breezy expanse of Rhode Island Sound. And, depending on the day and which hole you're playing, the wind can be all the obstacle a golfer can stand.

Good examples of that are the two opening holes, playing 377 yards and 180 yards, respectively, in a westerly direction, which means the prevailing southwesterly summer breezes can be a problem, not only serving to kill the distance you might hope for in your shots, but to push a modest fade into a full-blown slice.

The wind can be particularly disconcerting on #2, whose green not only abuts the rocky edge of Sakonnet River, but also is guarded on the left and right by four deep bunkers. And that same wind is hardly a help on the 404-yard 4th, a Scratch Par-4 that also plays almost due west.

The prevailing breeze can help on the 477-yard 3rd and the 364-yard 5th, both of which play in an easterly direction, but the same might not true of the 213-yard 6th, although it, too, runs east. The problems at #6 are near the green – mounds to the left, bunkers to the right, and a fall-off at the back – and the temptation of the recreational player is to play a wood from the tee. The frequent result of that strategy, of course, is that the unpredictable nature of woods, combined with the wind, can send the ball into one of the several trouble spots around the green, rather than safely onto the green. To persuade players to reconsider that temptation, Fair Par at Level 1 makes #6 a Par-4, with the extra stroke meant to give players the cushion to play an iron from the tee, with the front edge of the green, not the pin, as the target.

Sakonnet finishes with what is, perhaps, its prettiest hole, the 340-yard 18th, a well-bunkered beauty that plays toward the compound of weathered-shingle, white-trimmed cottages that make up Sakonnet's clubhouse buildings – as understated yet elegant a New England setting as any tourist, or golfer, could ask for.

Valley Country Club

New London Avenue, Warwick – 821-9621 – 18 holes

Scratch Par – 72
Fair Par Level 1 – 82
Fair Par Level 2 – 94

You can learn a lot about Valley by glancing at the handicap ratings for individual holes on the club's Scratch scorecard. What you'll find is that the number-one handicap hole on the front side is the longest on the course – #2, at 569 yards – and the top handicap hole on the back side is one of the shortest - #12, at 188 yards.

As odd as that might seem at first, it turns out not to be unusual at all, for if Valley is anything, it is a course of contrasts and surprises, a course that can be very flat or extremely rugged, a course where two holes share the same green, a course whose longer holes can be relatively trouble free while the shorter holes can be loaded with challenges that are sometimes subtle and sometimes decidedly not so.

Among Valley's strengths are its four shortest holes, all Scratch Par-3s, but none of them is easy.

The first of them is #6, which measures only 146 yards from the white tees, but plays uphill to a very small, severely sloping green that is bunkered both left and right. Next is the 200-yard 8th, which plays from an elevated tee to another sloping, well-bunkered green.

The toughest of the group is the aforementioned 12th, which requires a long carry from the tee, over a pond, to a green built on a hillside that slopes steeply back toward the water. Immediately adjacent is the 17th, 167 yards over the same pond, but in the opposite direction, and with just a little more forgiveness.

Of the four, two – #8 and #12 – can be considered candidates to be rated as four-shot holes at Fair Par Level 1, but only the 12th qualifies. Because the 8th plays from an elevated tee, not only does it play shorter than the yardage on the card, it gives players the psychological advantage of feeling that they don't have to really belt the ball to get it to the green, so the extra shot here is unnecessary.

On the 12th, the opposite is true. The hole tends to play longer than the yardage on the card, and, psychologically, the pond and the distance required to carry it can put players at a disadvantage. The extra stroke here is aimed getting players to relax a little on the tee in the face of the difficult shot ahead, and to encourage them to play just enough club to reach the front of the green.

In that way, a player will be less likely to spray the ball off the tee, perhaps slicing the ball into pond, which extends well to the right. He will also be more likely to keep the ball below the hole, something that is crucial, because the green slopes so severely toward the water that any putt hit from above the hole can run off the green, particularly in the summer, when the green can become wickedly slick.

In addition to these four holes, Valley boasts a number of other interesting and challenging holes, and one of the most dramatic is the 352-yard 11th. The hole features a fairway that drops into a valley off the tee and then runs uphill to the green. The fairway slopes in many directions, but predominantly to the left, and dense woods crowd in from both sides.

The trip to the green is a rough and tumble journey to be sure, and then the putting surface itself is a sloping, two-tiered affair that lies between green-side bunkers.

The 11th is a good example of how the length of a hole can be far less critical than its layout and topography, and that is reflected in the Fair Par rating, which sets the hole at a Par-5 at Level 1 and a Par-6 at Level 2. Despite its modest length, this is a hole that can break your heart if you're not careful, and the extra strokes provided by Fair Par are aimed at giving you the room to be careful.

Wannamoisett Country Club

96 Hoyt Avenue, Rumford – 434-9899 – 18 holes

Scratch Par – 69 men, 75 women
Fair Par Level 1 – 81
Fair Par Level 2 – 96

With a quiet cloak of green attempting to belie its fierce nature, Wannamoisett is nonetheless well known as one of the state's most intimidating tests of golf. The club was incorporated in 1898 and the course, which annually is included on lists of the country's top 100 courses, was designed in 1914 by Donald Ross. The PGA held its 1931 championship here, which Tom Creavy won by beating Walter Hagen, Tommy Armour and Gene Sarazen. The course has also been the annual site for the prestigious Northeast Amateur Invitational Tournament.

From the white tees, the course measures a hair under 6,400 yards, and from the blues the distance is 6,661, but Scratch Par is only 69, which tells you all you need to know about the problems a day at Wannamoisett poses for recreational players. It is no wonder, then, that the Fair Par allowances are generous here, as Level 1 gives golfers a 12-shot allowance over Scratch Par, and Level 2 players get a 27-shot cushion. Anyone who thinks those numbers might be excessive needs only play a few holes on the front side, and, in no time, he will find himself grateful for those shots, and maybe asking for even more.

The 1st, for example, is a 420-yard Scratch Par-4 that plays through a lovely stand of willow trees and over a pond that lies directly in front of the tee. Further along, players encounter a variety of mounds and bunkers both in the fairway and around the green.

Things get even more difficult on the 2nd, a 456-yard Scratch Par-4. Like many holes on the course, it begins as a hole with a wide open look and it is a relatively uncomplicated driving hole (depending, of course, on the cut of the often deep rough). But the closer you get to the green, the more trouble appears, as the fairway tightens between lines of trees, and bunkers begin to sprout with increasing frequency. Then, #2 adds a dramatic twist, as the fairway falls suddenly toward a stream that cuts across a few dozen yards in front of the green – a situation that puts a serious crimp in any plans a player might have for running up a second shot onto the green.

The 127-yard 3rd hole is a delight, but it comes as no surprise to anyone familiar with Donald Ross, who had a penchant for creating Scratch Par-3 holes that have steeply built-up perimeters around the green. This is one of those holes, a cheery little test that has the look of a raised up birthday cake with a single candle in the middle.

The party, such as it is, continues at #4, the highest rated handicap hole on the front side. At 440 yards, it starts as a fairly wide open driving hole, before bending a little to the left and narrowing between trees and bunkers as you approach the green.

There are two other rather lengthy Scratch Par-4 holes on the front side, #6 and #9, but it is the much shorter 7th, at 335 yards, that you are likely to remember more. While it might not look particularly troublesome from the tee, the fact is that the fairway erupts in rises, dips, slopes, and bunkers in the areas players are most likely to land their drives, and the front of the green is also well guarded by bunkers.

On the back nine, the length of the Scratch Par-4s moderates a bit, but the Scratch Par-3s grow a little longer, and the nine finishes with the 533-yard 17th, which features a two-tiered green, and the 416-yard 18th, which doglegs left and can be a very difficult driving hole for players who fade the ball.

One of the best holes on the back side is the 200-yard 12th, which plays somewhat uphill and features a huge bunker on the front right side of the sloping green. The green-side falls away hard on the left, and there are trees on the right and trouble behind. At Fair Par Level 1, the hole is a rated a Par-4 to encourage players to be patient and understand that whacking a wood could be a bad idea, while knocking an iron toward the front left edge of the green might be the smartest play.

Wanumetonomy Golf Club

152 Brown's Lane, Middletown – 847-3420 – 18 holes

Scratch Par – 70 men, 73 women
Fair Par Level 1 – 80
Fair Par Level 2 – 93

Wanumetonomy is said to have been the local Indian name describing a high place with a windy disposition, and that's appropriate for this course, for it is set on the side of a wide, breezy hill that slopes toward Narragansett Bay and gives the course much of its character.

Not only are there a number of holes that tend to play directly uphill or downhill, but also several holes play across the hillside, and their fairways are canted with the slope.

The hill also affects the greens, which can be slick and deceptively sloped – so much so that, on certain holes, players without local knowledge in reading the breaks can easily end up four-putting greens that, to the eye, seem relatively flat.

And then there is the wind, and plenty of it, generated by Wanumetonomy's proximity to the Bay.

Fortunately, those problematic natural elements are balanced by a layout that is neither excessively long nor particularly wooded, nor are there many water hazards to worry about. As at many of the state's private courses, the rough can get pretty deep, so the word to the wise at this golf course is a familiar one: keep the ball in the fairway and pray that your putter will be kind to you.

The course starts in a rather friendly fashion with a pair of holes that each measure only a dozen yards or so over 300 yards from the middle tees. The honeymoon ends abruptly, however, at the 3rd hole, which plays as a 453-yard, Scratch Par-4. It doesn't help that the hole also plays into the prevailing summer breeze. The good news is that it is fairly wide open up to the green, which is surrounded by bunkers.

As you might expect, #3 is rated as a Par-5 at Fair Par Level 1, and as a Par-6 at Level 2.

One of the best looking holes on the front side is the 5th, which plays 151 yards to a green that has the blue of Narragansett Bay as a backdrop. The hole is complicated by a small pond that lies to the left and front left of the green, and anyone being excessively shy of that hazard can quickly find the bunker on the right side of the green.

Perhaps the best hole on the golf course is the 10th, which plays 392 yards northward, across the face of the hillside, bending slightly to the right as it goes. Except for the sideways slope of the fairway, the tee shot is not a big problem, because the fairway is relatively wide. What does pose a problem is the approach to the green and the green itself.

First, the putting surface is raised above the fairway and the green-side falls off precipitously to the left and behind. Then, there are the bunkers, which lie all around the green. And, finally, the green is something of an optical illusion, looking relatively flat — that is, until you putt your ball and watch as it rolls to places you might never have expected.

Another among the difficult putting surfaces on the backside can be found on the 15th hole, which runs 399 yards slightly uphill to a green that is divided into three different tiers. Some members are fond of calling this the "Dolly Parton green," because the two higher tiers are separated by a cleavage that drops into the lower, flatter section. Depending on how devilish the greens keeper is feeling, there are places he can cut the hole that will guarantee almost everyone this side of Brad Faxon at least three putts.

The pleasant journey over Wanumetonomy finishes strongly with a 380-yard climb uphill over a rolling fairway that has a pronounced right-hand slope. The green is cut into the hillside, and falls away steeply, and predictably, on the right, a design that can easily send your final approach shot of the day bounding in direction you've no doubt become familiar with by this time — toward Narragansett Bay.

Warwick Country Club

Narragansett Bay Avenue, Warwick – 739-9878 – 18 holes

Scratch Par – 69 men, 73 women
Fair Par Level 1 – 80
Fair Par Level 2 – 93

Since the turn of the 20th century, Warwick Neck has been one the state's more upscale neighborhoods, as those who could afford it have come here to build elegant houses along the shores of Narragansett Bay.

A fixture in that neighborhood for most of that time has been Warwick Country Club, a lush, somewhat lengthy layout that meanders from the windy edge of the Bay up a gentle hillside to a park-like setting above, and then back to the shore in picturesque fashion.

The course has several characteristics that appear reliably on almost every hole. One is bunkers that are distinctive for being lumpy, bumpy, mounded affairs that bubble up from fairways and green-sides in great numbers. Another is the tendency of holes to start out as wide, inviting driving areas from the tees, and then to pinch in with trees and bunkers as you travel toward the green. Often, the constriction occurs in 200-240 yard range off the white tees, and it's not unusual for players to strike what seems like a strong, safe shot from the tee, only to find it has ended up in some fairway sand or behind a tree.

As noted, the course can play somewhat long, as it measures 6,269 yards from the white tees and 6,467 from the blues, and golfers are allowed only a paltry 69 shots to make Scratch Par. That sort of difficulty is evident on the opening hole, which, at 439 yards and running uphill, is the #1-rated handicap hole, as well as the longest, on the front nine.

It is far from the best hole on the nine, however. One hole contending for that honor is #5, a 406-yarder that runs generally downhill, sloping to the left while doglegging a bit to the right around a couple of fairway bunkers. More fairway bunkers and a solitary mound guard the approach to the green, and a line of trees pinches in from the right. The green itself is a two-tiered stage that is raised up from the fairway, and, as a result, the green-side falls away on the left and behind.

Number 5 is followed by two short but good-looking holes, the 331-yard 6th and the 182-yard 7th, but they prove only a set-up act for the big finish to the front side.

That begins at #8, a 378-yard hole that runs downhill between handsome lines of trees. From the tee, the white, gabled clubhouse is visible to the right of the distant green, and the background is filled with the blue of Narragansett Bay.

The finale is the beautiful but treacherous 165-yard 9th, which borders the Bay and plays over three small ponds. The hole is famous for being unpredictable, thanks to the strong winds that almost always blow hard off the water. Veterans of the hole will tell you they have hit everything from a wood to a wedge off the tee to compensate for the force and direction of the wind. And more than one golfer has misjudged the hole badly enough that they have flown drives into the clubhouse, which stands well behind the green.

The back nine – which begins almost exactly as the front did, with a 431-yard, uphill, Scratch Par-4 hole – turns out to be even longer than the front, boasting five holes measuring more than 400 yards, and only one of them, the 472-yard 15th, is listed as Scratch Par-5. One thing the two nines have in common is that the few holes that are short are among the tightest and most heavily bunkered. Another is that both sides finish well, the front with the signature 9th, and the back with a 417-yard trek that runs downhill toward the Bay between lines of trees. The drive on #18 can be problematic, for the fairway tightens with a bunker and trees in the area where average hitters might be landing drives. Bigger hitters can expect to fly that trouble, but they also must contend with a left-sloping fairway that can run a hooking ball into the trees.

The approach is interesting, because, although there are bunkers to both the left and right of the green and a steep fall-off behind, the front of the green is perfectly level with the fairway – an invitation for players to bump their second shots down the hill and run them up onto the green.

Executive, New, and Other Courses

Executive and Short Courses

Fairlawn Golf Course - 9 holes - Executive - Public
        Sherman Avenue, Lincoln - 334-3937

Foxwoods Executive GC at Lindhbrook - 9 holes - Executive - Public
        299 Woodville-Alton Road, Hope Valley - 539-8700

Silver Spring Golf Course - 6 holes - Public
        Pawtucket Avenue, East Providence - 434-9697

New and Developing Courses

Beaver River Golf Club - 18 holes - Public
        Route 138, Richmond - Opening: Fall 2000

Button Hole - 9 holes - Executive - Public (for children)
        King Phillip Road, Johnston/Providence - Opening: June, 2001

Cobblestone Hill Golf & Country Club - 18 holes - Public
        Route 102, Exeter - Opening: 2001

Carnegie Abbey - 18 holes - Private
        515 W. Main Rd., Portsmouth - 683-7720 - Open: July, 2000

Kingston Reserve - 18 holes - Public
        URI Campus, Kingston - Opening: 2002

Pinehurst Golf Club - 18 holes - Executive - Public
        Pinehurst Drive, Richmond - Opening: Spring 2001

Rose Hill Golf Club - 9 holes - Executive - Public
        Rose Hill Road, South Kingstown - Opening: Spring 2001

New and Proposed Courses

Scituate Highlands - 18 holes - Public
  Nipmuc Road, Scituate - Opening: Spring 2002

The Reserve at Brushy Brook - 18 holes - Public
  Dye Hill Road, Hope Valley - Opening: Summer 2001

Weaver Hill Country Club - 18 holes - Public
  Weaver Hill Road, Coventry - Opening: Spring 2002

Wentworth Hills Golf & Country Club - 18 holes - Semi-private
  27 Bow Street, Plainville, MA - 508-699-9406
  (5 holes lie in Cumberland, RI) - Opening: Fall 2000

Windmill Hill - 9 holes - Executive - Public
  School House Rd, Warren - 245-1463 - Opening: Spring 2000

Wood River Golf Course - 18 holes - Public
  Woodville-Alton Road, Hope Valley - Opening: June 2000

FAIR PAR SCORECARDS

(Note: To remove scorecards, tear along
perforation at spine. To remove a single card,
cut first along center line, as indicated.)

For more information and
additional scorecards contact:
www.fairpar.com
or 401-782-0324

Golfers and course operators are
encouraged to report changes in
course information to
Bogey Press
PO Box 5332
Wakefield RI 02880

Copyright © Stephen C. Heffner

Bristol Golf Club

Fair Par Level 1

—————— cut along line ——————

For more information and
additional scorecards contact:
www.fairpar.com
or 401-782-0324

Golfers and course operators are
encouraged to report changes in
course information to
Bogey Press
PO Box 5332
Wakefield RI 02880

Copyright © Stephen C. Heffner

Bristol Golf Club

Fair Par Level 2

Bristol Golf Club — Fair Par Level 1

Hole	Blue	White	Hcp.	Par	Red	Hcp.	+/-
1		137	7	3			
2		254	4	4			
3		148	9	3			
4		130	8	3			
5		167	6	3			
6		337	2	4			
7		480	1	6			
8		220	5	4			
9		224	3	4			
Out		2097		34			
10		137	7	3			
11		254	4	4			
12		148	9	3			
13		130	8	3			
14		167	6	3			
15		337	2	4			
16		480	1	6			
17		220	5	4			
18		224	3	4			
In		2097		34			
Total		4194		68			

— cut along line —

Bristol Golf Club — Fair Par Level 2

Hole	Blue	White	Hcp.	Par	Red	Hcp.	+/-
1		137	7	4			
2		254	4	5			
3		148	9	4			
4		130	8	4			
5		167	6	4			
6		337	2	5			
7		480	1	6			
8		220	5	4			
9		224	3	5			
Out		2097		41			
10		137	7	4			
11		254	4	5			
12		148	9	4			
13		130	8	4			
14		167	6	4			
15		337	2	5			
16		480	1	6			
17		220	5	4			
18		224	3	5			
In		2097		41			
Total		4194		82			

Country View Golf Club

Fair Par Level 1

cut along line

Country View Golf Club

Fair Par Level 2

Country View Golf Club — Fair Par Level 1

Hole	Blue	White	Hcp.	Par			Red	Hcp.	+/-
1	406	379	9	5			348	7	
2	291	281	11	4			275	15	
3	514	485	7	6			316	3	
4	189	178	15	3			164	17	
5	349	332	17	4			301	11	
6	398	392	1	5			331	1	
7	402	386	3	5			295	9	
8	199	184	13	3			160	13	
9	374	367	5	5			307	5	
Out	3122	2984		40			2547		
10	362	318	10	4			309	4	
11	141	126	18	3			119	16	
12	356	341	4	5			304	2	
13	365	347	6	4			292	8	
14	329	315	12	4			256	12	
15	475	461	14	6			392	6	
16	150	137	16	3			119	18	
17	381	344	2	4			256	14	
18	386	348	8	5			338	10	
In	2945	2737		38			2385		
Total	6067	5721		78			4932		

— cut along line —

Country View Golf Club — Fair Par Level 2

Hole	Blue	White	Hcp.	Par			Red	Hcp.	+/-
1	406	379	9	5			348	7	
2	291	281	11	5			275	15	
3	514	485	7	7			316	3	
4	189	178	15	4			164	17	
5	349	332	17	5			301	11	
6	398	392	1	6			331	1	
7	402	386	3	5			295	9	
8	199	184	13	4			160	13	
9	374	367	5	5			307	5	
Out	3122	2984		46			2547		
10	362	318	10	5			309	4	
11	141	126	18	4			119	16	
12	356	341	4	5			304	2	
13	365	347	6	5			292	8	
14	329	315	12	5			256	12	
15	475	461	14	7			392	6	
16	150	137	16	4			119	18	
17	381	344	2	5			256	14	
18	386	348	8	5			338	10	
In	2945	2737		45			2385		
Total	6067	5721		91			4932		

Coventry Pines Public GC

Fair Par Level 1

---

cut along line

Coventry Pines Public GC

Fair Par Level 2

Coventry Pines Public GC — Fair Par Level 1

Hole	Red	White	M. Hcp.	Par W/R	L. Hcp.	+/-
1	375	370	9	5	7	
2	308	303	17	4	13	
3	169	164	15	3	15	
4	484	430	3	5	5	
5	408	403	5	5	3	
6	520	515	1	6	1	
7	357	352	11	4	9	
8	187	182	7	3	17	
9	362	357	13	4	11	
Out	3170	3076		39		
10	375	370	10	5	8	
11	308	303	18	4	14	
12	169	164	16	3	16	
13	484	430	4	6	6	
14	408	403	6	5	4	
15	520	515	2	6	2	
16	357	352	12	4	10	
17	187	182	8	3	18	
18	362	357	14	4	12	
In	3170	3076		40		
Total	6340	6152		79		

cut along line

Coventry Pines Public GC — Fair Par Level 2

Hole	Red	White	M. Hcp.	Par W/R	L. Hcp.	+/-
1	375	370	9	5	7	
2	308	303	17	5	13	
3	169	164	15	4	15	
4	484	430	3	6	5	
5	408	403	5	6	3	
6	520	515	1	7	1	
7	357	352	11	5	9	
8	187	182	7	4	17	
9	362	357	13	5	11	
Out	3170	3076		47		
10	375	370	10	5	8	
11	308	303	18	5	14	
12	169	164	16	4	16	
13	484	430	4	6	6	
14	408	403	6	6	4	
15	520	515	2	7	2	
16	357	352	12	5	10	
17	187	182	8	4	18	
18	362	357	14	5	12	
In	3170	3076		47		
Total	6340	6152		94		

For more information and
additional scorecards contact:
www.fairpar.com
or 401-782-0324

Golfers and course operators are
encouraged to report changes in
course information to
Bogey Press
PO Box 5332
Wakefield RI 02880

Cranston
Country
Club

Fair Par
Level 1

--- cut along line ---

For more information and
additional scorecards contact:
www.fairpar.com
or 401-782-0324

Golfers and course operators are
encouraged to report changes in
course information to
Bogey Press
PO Box 5332
Wakefield RI 02880

Cranston
Country
Club

Fair Par
Level 2

Cranston Country Club — Fair Par Level 1

Hole	Blue	White	Hcp. B/W			Par			Red	Hcp.	+/-
1	543	529	9/1			6			450	3	
2	370	348	15/11			4			323	9	
3	395	375	13/17			5			355	15	
4	215	180	7/9			3			157	1	
5	408	346	5/7			5			305	17	
6	372	351	1/5			4			320	7	
7	366	344	17/13			4			322	11	
8	190	173	11/15			3			157	13	
9	457	410	3			5			344	5	
Out	3316	3056				39			2733		
10	385	345	8			5			305	8	
11	402	377	2/4			5			275	4	
12	141	125	18			3			100	18	
13	496	475	16/12			6			464	12	
14	373	349	14			4			304	14	
15	190	166	10/16			3			148	16	
16	388	369	12/10			5			347	10	
17	560	545	6/2			6			415	2	
18	385	355	4/6			5			305	6	
In	3320	3106				42			2663		
Total	6636	6162				81			5396		

cut along line

Cranston Country Club — Fair Par Level 2

Hole	Blue	White	Hcp. B/W			Par			Red	Hcp.	+/-
1	543	529	9/1			7			450	3	
2	370	348	15/11			5			323	9	
3	395	375	13/17			5			355	15	
4	215	180	7/9			4			157	1	
5	408	346	5/7			5			305	17	
6	372	351	1/5			5			320	7	
7	366	344	17/13			5			322	11	
8	190	173	11/15			4			157	13	
9	457	410	3			6			344	5	
Out	3316	3056				46			2733		
10	385	345	8			5			305	8	
11	402	377	2/4			6			275	4	
12	141	125	18			4			100	18	
13	496	475	16/12			7			464	12	
14	373	349	14			5			304	14	
15	190	166	10/16			4			148	16	
16	388	369	12/10			5			347	10	
17	560	545	6/2			7			415	2	
18	385	355	4/6			5			305	6	
In	3320	3106				48			2663		
Total	6636	6162				94			5396		

East Greenwich Golf & CC

Fair Par Level 1

For more information and
additional scorecards contact:
www.fairpar.com
or 401-782-0324

Golfers and course operators are
encouraged to report changes in
course information to
Bogey Press
PO Box 5332
Wakefield RI 02880

---

cut along line

East Greenwich Golf & CC

Fair Par Level 2

For more information and
additional scorecards contact:
www.fairpar.com
or 401-782-0324

Golfers and course operators are
encouraged to report changes in
course information to
Bogey Press
PO Box 5332
Wakefield RI 02880

East Greenwich Golf and Country Club — Fair Par Level 1

Hole	Blue	White	Hcp.	Par	Red	Hcp.	+/-
1	375	365	11	5	350	11	
2	345	325	13	4	310	13	
3	520	500	7	6	480	7	
4	390	360	9	4	340	9	
5	405	385	3	5	360	3	
6	135	130	17	3	120	17	
7	500	475	5	5	410	5	
8	400	380	1	5	360	1	
9	200	175	15	3	150	15	
Out	3270	3095		40	2880		
10	375	365	12	5	350	12	
11	345	325	14	4	310	14	
12	520	500	8	6	480	8	
13	390	360	10	4	340	10	
14	405	385	4	5	360	4	
15	135	130	18	3	120	18	
16	500	475	6	5	410	6	
17	400	380	2	5	360	2	
18	200	175	16	3	150	16	
In	3270	3095		40	2880		
Total	6540	6190		80	5760		

— cut along line —

East Greenwich Golf and Country Club — Fair Par Level 2

Hole	Blue	White	Hcp.	Par	Red	Hcp.	+/-
1	375	365	11	5	350	11	
2	345	325	13	5	310	13	
3	520	500	7	7	480	7	
4	390	360	9	5	340	9	
5	405	385	3	5	360	3	
6	135	130	17	4	120	17	
7	500	475	5	6	410	5	
8	400	380	1	6	360	1	
9	200	175	15	4	150	15	
Out	3270	3095		47	2880		
10	375	365	12	5	350	12	
11	345	325	14	5	310	14	
12	520	500	8	7	480	8	
13	390	360	10	5	340	10	
14	405	385	4	5	360	4	
15	135	130	18	4	120	18	
16	500	475	6	6	410	6	
17	400	380	2	6	360	2	
18	200	175	16	4	150	16	
In	3270	3095		47	2880		
Total	6540	6190		94	5760		

For more information and
additional scorecards contact:
www.fairpar.com
or 401-782-0324

Golfers and course operators are
encouraged to report changes in
course information to
Bogey Press
PO Box 5332
Wakefield RI 02880

Exeter Country Club

Fair Par Level 1

--- cut along line ---

For more information and
additional scorecards contact:
www.fairpar.com
or 401-782-0324

Golfers and course operators are
encouraged to report changes in
course information to
Bogey Press
PO Box 5332
Wakefield RI 02880

Exeter Country Club

Fair Par Level 2

Fair Par Level 1

Hole	Blue	White	Hcp.	Par	Red	Hcp.	+/-
1	377	350	9	5	300	13	
2	576	530	3	6	490	1	
3	219	190	13	3	170	17	
4	545	510	5	6	470	5	
5	217	180	17	3	150	15	
6	398	360	11	4	330	11	
7	462	420	1	5	390	7	
8	403	370	15	4	340	9	
9	431	400	7	5	370	3	
Out	3628	3310		41	3010		
10	422	400	8	5	370	2	
11	183	150	16	3	130	18	
12	357	330	18	4	310	14	
13	324	310	10	4	197	12	
14	497	480	4	6	460	4	
15	370	350	12	4	320	8	
16	396	370	2	5	296	10	
17	231	200	14	4	170	16	
18	511	490	6	6	470	6	
In	3291	3080		41	2723		
Total	6919	6390		82	5733		

Exeter Country Club

---- cut along line ----

Fair Par Level 2

Hole	Blue	White	Hcp.	Par	Red	Hcp.	+/-
1	377	350	9	5	300	13	
2	576	530	3	7	490	1	
3	219	190	13	4	170	17	
4	545	510	5	7	470	5	
5	217	180	17	4	150	15	
6	398	360	11	5	330	11	
7	462	420	1	6	390	7	
8	403	370	15	5	340	9	
9	431	400	7	5	370	3	
Out	3628	3310		48	3010		
10	422	400	8	5	370	2	
11	183	150	16	4	130	18	
12	357	330	18	5	310	14	
13	324	310	10	5	197	12	
14	497	480	4	6	460	4	
15	370	350	12	5	320	8	
16	396	370	2	6	296	10	
17	231	200	14	4	170	16	
18	511	490	6	6	470	6	
In	3291	3080		46	2723		
Total	6919	6390		94	5733		

Exeter Country Club

Fenner Hill
Golf Club

Fair Par
Level 1

cut along line

Fenner Hill
Golf Club

Fair Par
Level 2

Fenner Hill Golf Club

Hole	Blue	White	Gold	Hcp.	Par	Red	Hcp. (Fair Par Level 1)	+/-
1	380	366	350	13	5	338	13	
2	357	347	350	11	4	269	11	
3	520	486	324	5	6	407	5	
4	162	152	137	15	3	130	17	
5	371	352	337	7	5	301	7	
6	181	158	143	17	3	114	15	
7	429	394	368	1	5	362	3	
8	579	520	497	3	6	476	1	
9	370	355	340	9	5	290	9	
Out	3348	3111	2955		42	2687		
10	480	468	453	6	6	340	4	
11	180	164	142	14	3	105	18	
12	452	440	415	8	5	288	14	
13	352	338	307	12	4	290	6	
14	548	525	487	4	6	350	8	
15	325	309	292	16	4	282	12	
16	180	166	152	10	3	148	10	
17	315	297	280	18	4	267	16	
18	455	425	405	2	5	355	2	
In	3288	3132	2934		40	2405		
Total	6636	6263	5889		82	5112		

Fair Par Level 1

— cut along line —

Fenner Hill Golf Club

Hole	Blue	White	Gold	Hcp.	Par	Red	Hcp. (Fair Par Level 2)	+/-
1	380	366	350	13	5	338	13	
2	357	347	350	11	5	269	11	
3	520	486	324	5	6	407	5	
4	162	152	137	15	4	130	17	
5	371	352	337	7	5	301	7	
6	181	158	143	17	4	114	15	
7	429	394	368	1	5	362	3	
8	579	520	497	3	6	476	1	
9	370	355	340	9	5	290	9	
Out	3348	3111	2955		45	2687		
10	480	468	453	6	6	340	4	
11	180	164	142	14	4	105	18	
12	452	440	415	8	6	288	14	
13	352	338	307	12	5	290	6	
14	548	525	487	4	7	350	8	
15	325	309	292	16	5	282	12	
16	180	166	152	10	4	148	10	
17	315	297	280	18	5	267	16	
18	455	425	405	2	6	355	2	
In	3288	3132	2934		48	2405		
Total	6636	6263	5889		93	5112		

Fair Par Level 2

For more information and
additional scorecards contact:
www.fairpar.com
or 401-782-0324

Golfers and course operators are
encouraged to report changes in
course information to
Bogey Press
PO Box 5332
Wakefield RI 02880

Foster
Country
Club

Fair Par
Level 1

--------------------------------- cut along line ---------------------------------

For more information and
additional scorecards contact:
www.fairpar.com
or 401-782-0324

Golfers and course operators are
encouraged to report changes in
course information to
Bogey Press
PO Box 5332
Wakefield RI 02880

Foster
Country
Club

Fair Par
Level 2

Foster Country Club — Fair Par Level 1

Hole	Blue	White	Hcp.	Par	Red	Hcp.	+/-
1	356		5	5	350	5	
2	340		11	4	245	13	
3	241		9	4	230	15	
4	595		3	6	455	1	
5	295		13	4	285	9	
6	425		1	5	405	7	
7	130		17	3	125	17	
8	485		7	6	455	3	
9	310		15	4	300	11	
Out	3177			41	2850		
10	405		4	5	304	6	
11	310		16	4	285	14	
12	495		10	6	420	10	
13	375		2	5	300	2	
14	450		8	5	405	8	
15	295		12	4	290	12	
16	315		6	4	300	4	
17	170		18	3	160	18	
18	195		14	3	185	16	
In	3010			39	2649		
Total	6187			80	5499		

cut along line

Foster Country Club — Fair Par Level 2

Hole	Blue	White	Hcp.	Par	Red	Hcp.	+/-
1	356		5	5	350	5	
2	340		11	5	245	13	
3	241		9	4	230	15	
4	595		3	7	455	1	
5	295		13	5	285	9	
6	425		1	6	405	7	
7	130		17	4	125	17	
8	485		7	6	455	3	
9	310		15	5	300	11	
Out	3177			47	2850		
10	405		4	6	304	6	
11	310		16	5	285	14	
12	495		10	7	420	10	
13	375		2	5	300	2	
14	450		8	6	405	8	
15	295		12	5	290	12	
16	315		6	5	300	4	
17	170		18	4	160	18	
18	195		14	4	185	16	
In	3010			47	2649		
Total	6187			94	5499		

Foxwoods at Boulder Hills

Fair Par Level 1

---------------- cut along line ----------------

Foxwoods at Boulder Hills

Fair Par Level 2

Foxwoods at Boulder Hills — Fair Par Level 1

Hole	Blue	White	Hcp.	Par	Red	Hcp.	+/-
1	123	120	15	3	115	13	
2	319	290	9	4	280	5	
3	420	410	1	5	233	11	
4	498	465	5	6	325	3	
5	397	380	3	5	370	9	
6	120	107	17	3	95	17	
7	477	448	7	6	425	1	
8	151	137	13	3	130	15	
9	342	333	11	4	295	7	
Out	2847	2690		39	2268		
10	397	368	2	5	237	2	
11	367	344	6	5	270	4	
12	172	167	18	3	155	18	
13	346	331	10	4	325	8	
14	419	398	4	5	370	6	
15	496	430	14	5	416	12	
16	437	415	8	5	380	10	
17	359	331	12	4	320	14	
18	164	153	16	3	140	16	
In	3157	2937		39	2613		
Total	6004	5627		78	4881		

— cut along line —

Foxwoods at Boulder Hills — Fair Par Level 2

Hole	Blue	White	Hcp.	Par	Red	Hcp.	+/-
1	123	120	15	4	115	13	
2	319	290	9	5	280	5	
3	420	410	1	6	233	11	
4	498	465	5	7	325	3	
5	397	380	3	5	370	9	
6	120	107	17	4	95	17	
7	477	448	7	6	425	1	
8	151	137	13	4	130	15	
9	342	333	11	5	295	7	
Out	2847	2690		46	2268		
10	397	368	2	5	237	2	
11	367	344	6	5	270	4	
12	172	167	18	4	155	18	
13	346	331	10	5	325	8	
14	419	398	4	6	370	6	
15	496	430	14	6	416	12	
16	437	415	8	6	380	10	
17	359	331	12	5	320	14	
18	164	153	16	4	140	16	
In	3157	2937		46	2613		
Total	6004	5627		92	4881		

For more information and
additional scorecards contact:
www.fairpar.com
or 401-782-0324

Golfers and course operators are
encouraged to report changes in
course information to
Bogey Press
PO Box 5332
Wakefield RI 02880

Goddard Park GC

Fair Par Level 1

--------- cut along line ---------

For more information and
additional scorecards contact:
www.fairpar.com
or 401-782-0324

Golfers and course operators are
encouraged to report changes in
course information to
Bogey Press
PO Box 5332
Wakefield RI 02880

Goddard Park GC

Fair Par Level 2

Goddard Park GC — Fair Par Level 1

Hole	Blue	White	Hcp.	Par			Red	Hcp.	+/-
1		500	2	6					
2		375	4	5					
3		185	8	3					
4		286	7	5					
5		496	3	6					
6		300	5	4					
7		168	9	3					
8		390	1	5					
9		321	6	4					
Out		3021		40					
10		500	2	6					
11		375	4	5					
12		185	8	3					
13		286	7	4					
14		496	3	6					
15		300	5	4					
16		168	9	3					
17		390	1	5					
18		321	6	4					
In		3021		40					
Total		6042		80					

cut along line

Goddard Park GC — Fair Par Level 2

Hole	Blue	White	Hcp.	Par			Red	Hcp.	+/-
1		500	2	7					
2		375	4	5					
3		185	8	4					
4		286	7	5					
5		496	3	7					
6		300	5	5					
7		168	9	4					
8		390	1	5					
9		321	6	5					
Out		3021		47					
10		500	2	7					
11		375	4	5					
12		185	8	4					
13		286	7	5					
14		496	3	7					
15		300	5	5					
16		168	9	4					
17		390	1	5					
18		321	6	5					
In		3021		47					
Total		6042		94					

Green Valley CC

Fair Par
Level 1

---- cut along line ----

Green Valley CC

Fair Par
Level 2

Green Valley Country Club — Fair Par Level 1

Hole	Blue	White	Hcp.		Par			Red	Hcp.	+/-
1	370	361	15		5			331	17	
2	461	454	3		5			381	1	
3	397	386	7		5			329	11	
4	550	541	1		6			474	7	
5	190	175	11		3			125	9	
6	404	392	9		5			354	13	
7	360	354	13		4			314	3	
8	210	201	17		4			145	15	
9	433	424	5		5			361	5	
Out	3375	3288			42			2814		
10	613	605	2		6			466	12	
11	229	220	12		4			134	18	
12	147	125	18		3			101	16	
13	342	327	6		4			252	10	
14	451	440	10		5			332	2	
15	340	334	8		4			262	14	
16	407	394	16		5			336	4	
17	548	540	4		6			449	6	
18	378	368	14		4			313	8	
In	3455	3353			41			2645		
Total	6830	6641			83			5459		

— cut along line —

Green Valley Country Club — Fair Par Level 2

Hole	Blue	White	Hcp.		Par			Red	Hcp.	+/-
1	370	361	15		5			331	17	
2	461	454	3		6			381	1	
3	397	386	7		5			329	11	
4	550	541	1		7			474	7	
5	190	175	11		4			125	9	
6	404	392	9		5			354	13	
7	360	354	13		5			314	3	
8	210	201	17		4			145	15	
9	433	424	5		6			361	5	
Out	3375	3288			47			2814		
10	613	605	2		7			466	12	
11	229	220	12		4			134	18	
12	147	125	18		4			101	16	
13	342	327	6		5			252	10	
14	451	440	10		6			332	2	
15	340	334	8		5			262	14	
16	407	394	16		5			336	4	
17	548	540	4		7			449	6	
18	378	368	14		5			313	8	
In	3455	3353			48			2645		
Total	6830	6641			95			5459		

Jamestown Golf Course

Fair Par Level 1

cut along line

Jamestown Golf Course

Fair Par Level 2

Jamestown Golf Course — Fair Par Level 1

Hole	Blue	White	Hcp.	Par	Red	Hcp.	+/-
1		298	13	4	292	13	
2		541	1	6	510	1	
3		293	9	4	290	9	
4		388	7	5	370	7	
5		130	17	3	118	17	
6		450	5	6	395	5	
7		158	15	3	150	15	
8		405	3	5	369	3	
9		326	11	4	314	11	
Out		2989		40	2808		
10		298	14	4	292	14	
11		541	2	6	510	2	
12		293	10	4	290	10	
13		388	8	5	370	8	
14		130	18	3	118	18	
15		450	6	6	395	6	
16		158	16	3	150	16	
17		405	4	5	369	4	
18		326	12	4	314	12	
In		2989		40	2808		
Total		5978		80	5616		

----- cut along line -----

Jamestown Golf Course — Fair Par Level 2

Hole	Blue	White	Hcp.	Par	Red	Hcp.	+/-
1		298	13	5	292	13	
2		541	1	7	510	1	
3		293	9	5	290	9	
4		388	7	5	370	7	
5		130	17	4	118	17	
6		450	5	6	395	5	
7		158	15	4	150	15	
8		405	3	6	369	3	
9		326	11	5	314	11	
Out		2989		47	2808		
10		298	14	5	292	14	
11		541	2	7	510	2	
12		293	10	5	290	10	
13		388	8	5	370	8	
14		130	18	4	118	18	
15		450	6	6	395	6	
16		158	16	4	150	16	
17		405	4	6	369	4	
18		326	12	5	314	12	
In		2989		47	2808		
Total		5978		94	5616		

For more information and
additional scorecards contact:
www.fairpar.com
or 401-782-0324

Golfers and course operators are
encouraged to report changes in
course information to
Bogey Press
PO Box 5332
Wakefield RI 02880

Laurel
Lane
Golf Club

Fair Par
Level 1

--- cut along line ---

For more information and
additional scorecards contact:
www.fairpar.com
or 401-782-0324

Golfers and course operators are
encouraged to report changes in
course information to
Bogey Press
PO Box 5332
Wakefield RI 02880

Laurel
Lane
Golf Club

Fair Par
Level 2

Laurel Lane Golf Club — Fair Par Level 1

Hole	Blue	White	Hcp.			Par			Red	Hcp.	+/-
1	389	379	1			5			389	1	
2	480	470	9			6			440	9	
3	147	147	17			3			140	17	
4	363	363	11			4			323	3	
5	315	250	5			4			240	15	
6	245	245	13			5			115	13	
7	206	206	3			3			186	5	
8	320	320	15			4			290	11	
9	303	303	7			4			273	7	
Out	2768	2683				38			2396		
10	143	133	18			3			123	18	
11	472	462	10			6			422	4	
12	161	151	14			3			151	14	
13	538	528	2			6			440	2	
14	392	392	4			5			387	4	
15	317	317	12			5			310	6	
16	311	311	16			4			300	10	
17	323	323	6			4			318	8	
18	381	371	8			5			259	12	
In	3038	2988				41			2710		
Total	5806	5671				79			5106		

— cut along line —

Laurel Lane Golf Club — Fair Par Level 2

Hole	Blue	White	Hcp.			Par			Red	Hcp.	+/-
1	389	379	1			6			389	1	
2	480	470	9			6			440	9	
3	147	147	17			4			140	17	
4	363	363	11			5			323	3	
5	315	250	5			5			240	15	
6	245	245	13			5			115	13	
7	206	206	3			4			186	5	
8	320	320	15			5			290	11	
9	303	303	7			5			273	7	
Out	2768	2683				45			2396		
10	143	133	18			4			123	18	
11	472	462	10			7			422	4	
12	161	151	14			4			151	14	
13	538	528	2			7			440	2	
14	392	392	4			5			387	4	
15	317	317	12			5			310	6	
16	311	311	16			5			300	10	
17	323	323	6			5			318	8	
18	381	371	8			5			259	12	
In	3038	2988				47			2710		
Total	5806	5671				92			5106		

Meadowbrook Golf Course

Fair Par Level 1

cut along line

Meadowbrook Golf Course

Fair Par Level 2

Meadow Brook Golf Course — Fair Par Level 1

Hole	Blue	White	Hcp.	Par	Red	Hcp.	+/-
1		300	13	4	245	13	
2		175	15	3	155	15	
3		350	7	5	335	7	
4		335	9	4	325	9	
5		155	17	3	140	17	
6		535	1	6	475	1	
7		300	11	4	290	11	
8		365	5	5	355	5	
9		505	3	6	420	3	
Out		3020		40	2740		
10		180	16	3	155	16	
11		385	8	5	385	8	
12		350	14	4	290	14	
13		485	2	6	475	2	
14		395	6	5	350	6	
15		385	10	4	375	10	
16		340	12	4	330	12	
17		395	4	5	385	4	
18		140	18	3	120	18	
In		3055		39	2865		
Total		6075		79	5605		

cut along line

Meadow Brook Golf Course — Fair Par Level 2

Hole	Blue	White	Hcp.	Par	Red	Hcp.	+/-
1		300	13	5	245	13	
2		175	15	4	155	15	
3		350	7	5	335	7	
4		335	9	5	325	9	
5		155	17	4	140	17	
6		535	1	7	475	1	
7		300	11	5	290	11	
8		365	5	5	355	5	
9		505	3	6	420	3	
Out		3020		46	2740		
10		180	16	4	155	16	
11		385	8	5	385	8	
12		350	14	5	290	14	
13		485	2	6	475	2	
14		395	6	5	350	6	
15		385	10	5	375	10	
16		340	12	5	330	12	
17		395	4	5	385	4	
18		140	18	4	120	18	
In		3055		44	2865		
Total		6075		90	5605		

Melody Hill GC

Fair Par Level 1

---

cut along line

Melody Hill GC

Fair Par Level 2

Melody Hill Golf Course — Fair Par Level 1

Hole	Blue	White	Hcp.	Par	Red	Hcp.	+/-
1		360	10	4			
2		315	13	4			
3		385	8	5			
4		95	18	3			
5		465	3	5			
6		145	17	3			
7		425	5	5			
8		500	1	6			
9		235	14	4			
Out		2925		39			
10		445	2	6			
11		405	6	5			
12		535	4	6			
13		185	15	3			
14		360	11	4			
15		165	16	3			
16		355	12	4			
17		400	7	5			
18		410	9	5			
In		3260		41			
Total		6185		80			

— cut along line —

Melody Hill Golf Course — Fair Par Level 2

Hole	Blue	White	Hcp.	Par	Red	Hcp.	+/-
1		360	10	5			
2		315	13	5			
3		385	8	5			
4		95	18	3			
5		465	3	6			
6		145	17	4			
7		425	5	6			
8		500	1	7			
9		235	14	4			
Out		2925		45			
10		445	2	6			
11		405	6	6			
12		535	4	7			
13		185	15	4			
14		360	11	5			
15		165	16	4			
16		355	12	5			
17		400	7	6			
18		410	9	5			
In		3260		48			
Total		6185		93			

For more information and
additional scorecards contact:
www.fairpar.com
or 401-782-0324

Golfers and course operators are
encouraged to report changes in
course information to
Bogey Press
PO Box 5332
Wakefield RI 02880

Midville Country Club

Fair Par Level 1

---

cut along line

For more information and
additional scorecards contact:
www.fairpar.com
or 401-782-0324

Golfers and course operators are
encouraged to report changes in
course information to
Bogey Press
PO Box 5332
Wakefield RI 02880

Midville Country Club

Fair Par Level 2

Fair Par Level 1

Hole	Blue	White	Hcp. W/B			Par W/B		Red	Hcp.	+/-
1	359	334	7			4		324	7	
2	321	314	5			4		235	5	
3	343	327	3			4		292	3	
4	378	346	9			5		300	9	
5	171	145	17			3		122	17	
6	540	523	1			6		492	1	
7	168	145	15			3		111	15	
8	344	309	13			4		215	13	
9	346	336	11			4		249	11	
Out	2970	2779				37		2340		
10	359	334	12			5		324	12	
11	321	314	10			5		235	10	
12	343	327	6			4		292	6	
13	378	346	4			5		300	4	
14	171	145	18			3		122	18	
15	540	523	2			6		492	2	
16	168	145	14			3		111	14	
17	344	309	8			4		215	8	
18	346	336	16			5		249	16	
In	2970	2779				40		2340		
Total	5940	5558				77		4680		

Midville Country Club

— cut along line —

Fair Par Level 2

Hole	Blue	White	Hcp. W/B			Par W/B		Red	Hcp.	+/-
1	359	334	7			5		324	7	
2	321	314	5			5		235	5	
3	343	327	3			5		292	3	
4	378	346	9			5		300	9	
5	171	145	17			4		122	17	
6	540	523	1			7		492	1	
7	168	145	15			4		111	15	
8	344	309	13			5		215	13	
9	346	336	11			5		249	11	
Out	2970	2779				45		2340		
10	359	334	12			5		324	12	
11	321	314	10			5		235	10	
12	343	327	6			5		292	6	
13	378	346	4			5		300	4	
14	171	145	18			4		122	18	
15	540	523	2			7		492	2	
16	168	145	14			4		111	14	
17	344	309	8			5		215	8	
18	346	336	16			5		249	16	
In	2970	2779				45		2340		
Total	5940	5558				90		4680		

Midville Country Club

For more information and
additional scorecards contact:
www.fairpar.com
or 401-782-0324

Golfers and course operators are
encouraged to report changes in
course information to
Bogey Press
PO Box 5332
Wakefield RI 02880

Montaup Country Club

Fair Par Level 1

cut along line

For more information and
additional scorecards contact:
www.fairpar.com
or 401-782-0324

Golfers and course operators are
encouraged to report changes in
course information to
Bogey Press
PO Box 5332
Wakefield RI 02880

Montaup Country Club

Fair Par Level 2

Montaup Country Club — Fair Par Level 1

Hole	Blue	White	Hcp.		Par		Red	Hcp.	+/-
1	413	398	3		5		401	3	
2	399	399	7		5		338	5	
3	219	211	9		4		131	17	
4	391	381	11		5		357	9	
5	527	468	1		6		401	7	
6	360	342	13		4		297	11	
7	561	505	5		6		429	1	
8	152	137	15		3		90	15	
9	334	325	17		4		325	13	
Out	3356	3166			42		2769		
10	159	148	12		3		138	14	
11	408	394	6		5		344	16	
12	187	175	14		3		165	12	
13	513	505	10		6		420	2	
14	166	156	16		3		138	18	
15	431	395	2		5		401	4	
16	518	445	8		6		440	6	
17	404	333	4		4		324	10	
18	304	293	18		4		293	8	
In	3090	2844			39		2663		
Total	6446	6010			81		5432		

— cut along line —

Montaup Country Club — Fair Par Level 2

Hole	Blue	White	Hcp.		Par		Red	Hcp.	+/-
1	413	398	3		6		401	3	
2	399	399	7		6		338	5	
3	219	211	9		4		131	17	
4	391	381	11		5		357	9	
5	527	468	1		7		401	7	
6	360	342	13		5		297	11	
7	561	505	5		7		429	1	
8	152	137	15		4		90	15	
9	334	325	17		5		325	13	
Out	3356	3166			49		2769		
10	159	148	12		4		138	14	
11	408	394	6		6		344	16	
12	187	175	14		4		165	12	
13	513	505	10		7		420	2	
14	166	156	16		4		138	18	
15	431	395	2		5		401	4	
16	518	445	8		6		440	6	
17	404	333	4		6		324	10	
18	304	293	18		5		293	8	
In	3090	2844			47		2663		
Total	6446	6010			96		5432		

North Kingstown GC

Fair Par Level 1

For more information and additional scorecards contact:
www.fairpar.com
or 401-782-0324

Golfers and course operators are encouraged to report changes in course information to
Bogey Press
PO Box 5332
Wakefield RI 02880

---

cut along line

North Kingstown GC

Fair Par Level 2

For more information and additional scorecards contact:
www.fairpar.com
or 401-782-0324

Golfers and course operators are encouraged to report changes in course information to
Bogey Press
PO Box 5332
Wakefield RI 02880

North Kingstown Golf Course — Fair Par Level 1

Hole	Blue	White	Hcp.	Par	Red	Hcp.	+/-
1	369	354	11	5	339	11	
2	411	392	1	5	385	1	
3	185	154	15	3	137	15	
4	499	448	9	5	425	5	
5	375	362	7	5	348	9	
6	353	343	5	5	263	7	
7	545	483	3	6	441	3	
8	197	171	13	3	157	17	
9	283	276	17	4	269	13	
Out	3217	2983		41	2764		
10	171	159	16	3	148	18	
11	559	551	6	6	433	4	
12	333	321	10	4	260	10	
13	403	392	8	5	348	8	
14	194	188	14	3	157	14	
15	413	403	2	5	352	2	
16	398	388	4	5	378	6	
17	315	304	12	4	259	12	
18	158	139	18	3	128	16	
In	2944	2845		38	2463		
Total	6161	5828		79	5227		

cut along line

North Kingstown Golf Course — Fair Par Level 2

Hole	Blue	White	Hcp.	Par	Red	Hcp.	+/-
1	369	354	11	5	339	11	
2	411	392	1	5	385	1	
3	185	154	15	4	137	15	
4	499	448	9	6	425	5	
5	375	362	7	5	348	9	
6	353	343	5	5	263	7	
7	545	483	3	7	441	3	
8	197	171	13	4	157	17	
9	283	276	17	5	269	13	
Out	3217	2983		46	2764		
10	171	159	16	4	148	18	
11	559	551	6	7	433	4	
12	333	321	10	5	260	10	
13	403	392	8	5	348	8	
14	194	188	14	4	157	14	
15	413	403	2	6	352	2	
16	398	388	4	5	378	6	
17	315	304	12	5	259	12	
18	158	139	18	4	128	16	
In	2944	2845		45	2463		
Total	6161	5828		91	5227		

For more information and
additional scorecards contact:
www.fairpar.com
or 401-782-0324

Golfers and course operators are
encouraged to report changes in
course information to
Bogey Press
PO Box 5332
Wakefield RI 02880

Copyright © Stephen C. Heffner

Pocasset Country Club

Fair Par Level 1

cut along line

For more information and
additional scorecards contact:
www.fairpar.com
or 401-782-0324

Golfers and course operators are
encouraged to report changes in
course information to
Bogey Press
PO Box 5332
Wakefield RI 02880

Copyright © Stephen C. Heffner

Pocasset Country Club

Fair Par Level 2

Pocasset Country Club — Fair Par Level 1

Hole	Blue	White	Hcp.	Par	Red	Hcp.	+/-
1		305	13	4	305	13	
2		395	5	5	380	5	
3		210	9	4	210	9	
4		275	17	4	275	17	
5		385	3	4	385	3	
6		195	7	4	155	7	
7		275	15	4	260	15	
8		330	11	4	220	11	
9		425	1	5	425	1	
Out		2795		38	2615		
10		305	14	4	305	14	
11		395	6	5	380	6	
12		210	10	4	210	10	
13		275	18	4	275	18	
14		385	4	4	385	4	
15		195	8	4	155	8	
16		275	16	4	260	16	
17		330	12	4	22	12	
18		425	2	5	425	2	
In		2795		38	2615		
Total		5590		76	5230		

— cut along line —

Pocasset Country Club — Fair Par Level 2

Hole	Blue	White	Hcp.	Par	Red	Hcp.	+/-
1		305	13	5	305	13	
2		395	5	5	380	5	
3		210	9	4	210	9	
4		275	17	5	275	17	
5		385	3	5	385	3	
6		195	7	4	155	7	
7		275	15	5	260	15	
8		330	11	5	220	11	
9		425	1	6	425	1	
Out		2795		44	2615		
10		305	14	5	305	14	
11		395	6	5	380	6	
12		210	10	4	210	10	
13		275	18	5	275	18	
14		385	4	4	385	4	
15		195	8	5	155	8	
16		275	16	5	260	16	
17		330	12	5	22	12	
18		425	2	6	425	2	
In		2795		44	2615		
Total		5590		88	5230		

For more information and
additional scorecards contact:
www.fairpar.com
or 401-782-0324

Golfers and course operators are
encouraged to report changes in
course information to
Bogey Press
PO Box 5332
Wakefield RI 02880

Richmond
Country
Club

Fair Par
Level 1

---------- cut along line ----------

For more information and
additional scorecards contact:
www.fairpar.com
or 401-782-0324

Golfers and course operators are
encouraged to report changes in
course information to
Bogey Press
PO Box 5332
Wakefield RI 02880

Richmond
Country
Club

Fair Par
Level 2

Richmond Country Club — Fair Par Level 1

Hole	Gold	Blue	White	Hcp.	Par	Red	Hcp.	+/-
1	453	381	318	9	4	239	13	
2	449	388	353	5	5	298	5	
3	259	259	204	13	4	149	11	
4	594	557	504	1	6	450	3	
5	167	167	165	17	3	121	17	
6	452	452	428	3	5	358	1	
7	501	501	450	7	6	418	7	
8	324	324	277	15	4	234	15	
9	333	333	285	11	4	285	9	
Out	3532	3362	2984		41	2552		
10	441	378	320	14	4	247	8	
11	480	480	431	10	6	386	10	
12	211	211	184	16	3	184	14	
13	439	439	408	2	5	338	12	
14	423	399	368	6	5	325	4	
15	230	198	176	8	3	152	16	
16	542	520	474	4	6	412	2	
17	173	173	154	18	3	115	18	
18	355	355	328	12	4	263	6	
In	3294	3153	2843		39	2422		
Total	6826	6515	5827		80	4974		

— cut along line —

Richmond Country Club — Fair Par Level 2

Hole	Gold	Blue	White	Hcp.	Par	Red	Hcp.	+/-
1	453	381	318	9	5	239	13	
2	449	388	353	5	5	298	5	
3	259	259	204	13	4	149	11	
4	594	557	504	1	7	450	3	
5	167	167	165	17	4	121	17	
6	452	452	428	3	6	358	1	
7	501	501	450	7	6	418	7	
8	324	324	277	15	5	234	15	
9	333	333	285	11	5	285	9	
Out	3532	3362	2984		47	2552		
10	441	378	320	14	5	247	8	
11	480	480	431	10	6	386	10	
12	211	211	184	16	4	184	14	
13	439	439	408	2	6	338	12	
14	423	399	368	6	5	325	4	
15	230	198	176	8	4	152	16	
16	542	520	474	4	7	412	2	
17	173	173	154	18	4	115	18	
18	355	355	328	12	5	263	6	
In	3294	3153	2843		46	2422		
Total	6826	6515	5827		93	4974		

Rolling Greens GC

Fair Par Level 1

cut along line

Rolling Greens GC

Fair Par Level 2

Rolling Greens Golf Course — Fair Par Level 1

Hole	Blue	White	Hcp.		Par		Red	Hcp.	+/-
1		339	13		4				
2		353	7		5				
3		383	3		5				
4		147	17		3				
5		550	5		6				
6		325	9		4				
7		315	11		4				
8		220	15		3				
9		440	1		5				
Out		3072			39				
10		339	14		4				
11		353	8		5				
12		383	4		5				
13		147	18		3				
14		550	6		6				
15		325	10		4				
16		315	12		4				
17		220	16		3				
18		440	2		5				
In		3072			39				
Total		6144			78				

cut along line

Rolling Greens Golf Course — Fair Par Level 2

Hole	Blue	White	Hcp.		Par		Red	Hcp.	+/-
1		339	13		5				
2		353	7		5				
3		383	3		5				
4		147	17		4				
5		550	5		7				
6		325	9		5				
7		315	11		5				
8		220	15		4				
9		440	1		6				
Out		3072			46				
10		339	14		5				
11		353	8		5				
12		383	4		5				
13		147	18		4				
14		550	6		7				
15		325	10		5				
16		315	12		5				
17		220	16		4				
18		440	2		6				
In		3072			46				
Total		6144			92				

For more information and
additional scorecards contact:
www.fairpar.com
or 401-782-0324

Golfers and course operators are
encouraged to report changes in
course information to
Bogey Press
PO Box 5332
Wakefield RI 02880

Copyright © Stephen C. Heffner

Seaview Country Club

Fair Par Level 1

cut along line

For more information and
additional scorecards contact:
www.fairpar.com
or 401-782-0324

Golfers and course operators are
encouraged to report changes in
course information to
Bogey Press
PO Box 5332
Wakefield RI 02880

Copyright © Stephen C. Heffner

Seaview Country Club

Fair Par Level 2

Seaview Country Club — Par — Fair Par Level 1

Hole	Blue	White	Hcp.	Par	Red	Hcp.	+/-
1	305		7	4	295	7	
2	274		13	4	254	13	
3	282		15	4	201	15	
4	551		1	6	526	1	
5	143		17	3	123	17	
6	201		3	4	151	3	
7	302		9	4	282	9	
8	350		5	4	290	5	
9	495		11	6	455	11	
Out	2903			39	2577		
10	305		8	4	295	8	
11	274		14	4	254	14	
12	242		16	4	201	16	
13	551		2	6	526	2	
14	143		18	3	123	18	
15	201		4	4	151	4	
16	302		10	4	282	10	
17	310		6	4	290	6	
18	495		12	6	455	12	
In	2823			39	2577		
Total	5806			78	5154		

cut along line

Seaview Country Club — Par — Fair Par Level 2

Hole	Blue	White	Hcp.	Par	Red	Hcp.	+/-
1	305		7	5	295	7	
2	274		13	5	254	13	
3	282		15	5	201	15	
4	551		1	7	526	1	
5	143		17	4	123	17	
6	201		3	4	151	3	
7	302		9	5	282	9	
8	350		5	5	290	5	
9	495		11	6	455	11	
Out	2903			46	2577		
10	305		8	5	295	8	
11	274		14	5	254	14	
12	242		16	5	201	16	
13	551		2	7	526	2	
14	143		18	4	123	18	
15	201		4	4	151	4	
16	302		10	5	282	10	
17	310		6	5	290	6	
18	495		12	6	455	12	
In	2823			46	2577		
Total	5806			92	5154		

Triggs Memorial GC

Fair Par Level 1

---

cut along line

Triggs Memorial GC

Fair Par Level 2

Triggs Mem. Golf Course — Fair Par Level 1

Hole	Blue	White	Hcp.	Par	Red	Hcp.	+/-
1	402	379	9	5	362	9	
2	425	411	3	5	352	5	
3	457	445	1	5	369	7	
4	200	184	17	3	167	17	
5	327	316	11	4	313	3	
6	445	437	7	6	431	1	
7	191	185	15	3	135	15	
8	341	332	13	4	285	13	
9	402	391	5	5	359	11	
Out	3190	3080		40	2773		
10	513	502	8	6	480	2	
11	350	340	10	4	332	4	
12	200	195	16	3	146	18	
13	462	447	12	6	381	6	
14	158	140	18	3	126	16	
15	508	496	4	6	380	8	
16	319	302	14	4	187	14	
17	412	401	2	5	273	12	
18	410	399	6	5	314	10	
In	3332	3222		42	2619		
Total	6522	6302		82	5392		

—— cut along line ——

Triggs Mem. Golf Course — Fair Par Level 2

Hole	Blue	White	Hcp.	Par	Red	Hcp.	+/-
1	402	379	9	5	362	9	
2	425	411	3	6	352	5	
3	457	445	1	6	369	7	
4	200	184	17	4	167	17	
5	327	316	11	5	313	3	
6	445	437	7	6	431	1	
7	191	185	15	4	135	15	
8	341	332	13	5	285	13	
9	402	391	5	5	359	11	
Out	3190	3080		46	2773		
10	513	502	8	7	480	2	
11	350	340	10	5	332	4	
12	200	195	16	4	146	18	
13	462	447	12	7	381	6	
14	158	140	18	4	126	16	
15	508	496	4	7	380	8	
16	319	302	14	5	187	14	
17	412	401	2	6	273	12	
18	410	399	6	6	314	10	
In	3332	3222		51	2619		
Total	6522	6302		97	5392		

Washington Village GC

Fair Par

Level 1

---- cut along line ----

Washington Village GC

Fair Par

Level 2

Washington Village GC — Fair Par Level 1

Hole	Blue	White	Hcp.			Par			Fair Par Level 1	Red	Hcp.	+/-
1	175	170	6			3				74	9	
2	360	350	1			5				317	1	
3	150	135	8			3				78	7	
4	310	300	9			4				268	4	
5	470	450	2			6				390	2	
6	200	185	4			3				178	5	
7	360	350	3			5				297	3	
8	200	175	5			3				168	6	
9	300	290	7			4				223	8	
Out	2525	2405				36				1993		
10	175	170	15			3				74	18	
11	360	350	10			5				317	10	
12	150	135	17			3				78	16	
13	310	300	18			4				268	13	
14	470	450	11			6				390	11	
15	200	185	13			3				178	14	
16	360	350	12			5				297	12	
17	200	175	14			3				168	15	
18	300	290	16			4				223	17	
In	2525	2405				36				1993		
Total	5050	4810				72				3986		

— cut along line —

Washington Village GC — Fair Par Level 2

Hole	Blue	White	Hcp.			Par			Fair Par Level 2	Red	Hcp.	+/-
1	175	170	6			4				74	9	
2	360	350	1			5				317	1	
3	150	135	8			4				78	7	
4	310	300	9			5				268	4	
5	470	450	2			6				390	2	
6	200	185	4			4				178	5	
7	360	350	3			5				297	3	
8	200	175	5			4				168	6	
9	300	290	7			5				223	8	
Out	2525	2405				42				1993		
10	175	170	15			4				74	18	
11	360	350	10			5				317	10	
12	150	135	17			4				78	16	
13	310	300	18			5				268	13	
14	470	450	11			6				390	11	
15	200	185	13			4				178	14	
16	360	350	12			5				297	12	
17	200	175	14			4				168	15	
18	300	290	16			5				223	17	
In	2525	2405				42				1993		
Total	5050	4810				84				3986		

Weekapaug Golf Club

Fair Par
Level 1

---- cut along line ----

Weekapaug Golf Club

Fair Par
Level 2

Weekapaug Golf Club

Fair Par Level 1

Hole	Blue	White	Hcp.	Par B/W	Red	Hcp.	+/-
1	418	410	3	5	329	3	
2	340	336	15	4	280	15	
3	185	176	9	4	154	9	
4	352	342	5	5	317	7	
5	474	466	13	5	364	13	
6	424	417	1	5	333	1	
7	378	371	11	4	342	11	
8	130	121	17	3	115	17	
9	519	512	7	6	413	5	
Out	3220	3151		41	2647		
10	418	410	4	5	329	4	
11	340	336	16	4	280	16	
12	185	176	10	3	154	10	
13	352	342	6	5	317	8	
14	474	466	14	5	364	14	
15	424	417	2	5	333	2	
16	378	371	12	4	342	12	
17	130	121	18	3	115	18	
18	519	512	8	6	413	6	
In	3220	3151		40	2647		
Total	6440	6302		81	5294		

cut along line

Weekapaug Golf Club

Fair Par Level 2

Hole	Blue	White	Hcp.	Par	Red	Hcp.	+/-
1	418	410	3	6	329	3	
2	340	336	15	5	280	15	
3	185	176	9	4	154	9	
4	352	342	5	5	317	7	
5	474	466	13	6	364	13	
6	424	417	1	6	333	1	
7	378	371	11	5	342	11	
8	130	121	17	4	115	17	
9	519	512	7	7	413	5	
Out	3220	3151		48	2647		
10	418	410	4	6	329	4	
11	340	336	16	5	280	16	
12	185	176	10	4	154	10	
13	352	342	6	5	317	8	
14	474	466	14	6	364	14	
15	424	417	2	6	333	2	
16	378	371	12	5	342	12	
17	130	121	18	4	115	18	
18	519	512	8	7	413	6	
In	3220	3151		48	2647		
Total	6440	6302		96	5294		

For more information and
additional scorecards contact:
www.fairpar.com
or 401-782-0324

Golfers and course operators are
encouraged to report changes in
course information to
Bogey Press
PO Box 5332
Wakefield RI 02880

West Warwick CC

Fair Par Level 1

cut along line

For more information and
additional scorecards contact:
www.fairpar.com
or 401-782-0324

Golfers and course operators are
encouraged to report changes in
course information to
Bogey Press
PO Box 5332
Wakefield RI 02880

West Warwick CC

Fair Par Level 2

West Warwick Country Club — Fair Par Level 1

Hole	Blue	White	Hcp.	Par		Red	Hcp.	+/-
1		419	1	5		419	1	
2		338	13	4		302	3	
3		140	15	3		114	13	
4		375	3	5		341	5	
5		365	5	4		365	7	
6		360	9	5		360	9	
7		333	11	4		333	11	
8		162	17	3		150	15	
9		509	7	6		384	17	
Out		3001		39		2768		
10		419	2	5		419	2	
11		338	14	4		302	4	
12		140	16	3		114	14	
13		375	4	5		341	6	
14		365	6	4		365	8	
15		360	10	5		360	10	
16		333	12	4		333	12	
17		162	18	3		150	16	
18		509	8	6		384	18	
In		3001		39		2768		
Total		6002		78		5536		

— cut along line —

West Warwick Country Club — Fair Par Level 2

Hole	Blue	White	Hcp.	Par		Red	Hcp.	+/-
1		419	1	6		419	1	
2		338	13	5		302	3	
3		140	15	4		114	13	
4		375	3	6		341	5	
5		365	5	5		365	7	
6		360	9	5		360	9	
7		333	11	5		333	11	
8		162	17	4		150	15	
9		509	7	7		384	17	
Out		3001		47		2768		
10		419	2	6		419	2	
11		338	14	5		302	4	
12		140	16	4		114	14	
13		375	4	6		341	6	
14		365	6	5		365	8	
15		360	10	5		360	10	
16		333	12	5		333	12	
17		162	18	4		150	16	
18		509	8	7		384	18	
In		3001		47		2768		
Total		6002		94		5536		

For more information and
additional scorecards contact:
www.fairpar.com
or 401-782-0324

Golfers and course operators are
encouraged to report changes in
course information to
Bogey Press
PO Box 5332
Wakefield RI 02880

Winnapaug Country Club

Fair Par Level 1

---

cut along line

For more information and
additional scorecards contact:
www.fairpar.com
or 401-782-0324

Golfers and course operators are
encouraged to report changes in
course information to
Bogey Press
PO Box 5332
Wakefield RI 02880

Winnapaug Country Club

Fair Par Level 2

Fair Par Level 1 / Winnapaug Country Club

Hole	Blue	White	Hcp.		Par		Red	Hcp.	+/-
1	339	319	15		4		251	16	
2	496	480	11		6		391	6	
3	169	156	5		3		138	12	
4	425	402	1		5		359	2	
5	338	282	9		4		270	14	
6	127	110	17		3		90	18	
7	356	344	13		5		261	10	
8	355	307	3		4		291	8	
9	525	480	7		6		403	4	
Out	3130	2880			40		2454		
10	405	395	4		5		390	3	
11	352	348	8		4		298	11	
12	167	141	12		3		135	15	
13	487	472	16		6		388	9	
14	405	383	2		5		360	1	
15	461	451	6		5		395	5	
16	179	150	18		3		140	17	
17	435	392	10		5		371	7	
18	340	302	14		4		222	13	
In	3231	3034			40		2699		
Total	6361	5914			80		5153		

— cut along line —

Fair Par Level 2 / Winnapaug Country Club

Hole	Blue	White	Hcp.		Par		Red	Hcp.	+/-
1	339	319	15		5		251	16	
2	496	480	11		7		391	6	
3	169	156	5		4		138	12	
4	425	402	1		6		359	2	
5	338	282	9		5		270	14	
6	127	110	17		4		90	18	
7	356	344	13		5		261	10	
8	355	307	3		5		291	8	
9	525	480	7		6		403	4	
Out	3130	2880			47		2454		
10	405	395	4		5		390	3	
11	352	348	8		5		298	11	
12	167	141	12		4		135	15	
13	487	472	16		6		388	9	
14	405	383	2		5		360	1	
15	461	451	6		6		395	5	
16	179	150	18		4		140	17	
17	435	392	10		5		371	7	
18	340	302	14		5		222	13	
In	3231	3034			45		2699		
Total	6361	5914			92		5153		

For more information and
additional scorecards contact:
www.fairpar.com
or 401-782-0324

Golfers and course operators are
encouraged to report changes in
course information to
Bogey Press
PO Box 5332
Wakefield RI 02880

Copyright © Stephen C. Heffner

Woodland Greens Golf Club

Fair Par Level 1

---

cut along line

For more information and
additional scorecards contact:
www.fairpar.com
or 401-782-0324

Golfers and course operators are
encouraged to report changes in
course information to
Bogey Press
PO Box 5332
Wakefield RI 02880

Copyright © Stephen C. Heffner

Woodland Greens Golf Club

Fair Par Level 2

Woodland Greens GC — Fair Par Level 1

Hole	Blue	White	Hcp.	Par W/B	Red	Hcp.	+/-
1	370	360	7	5	350	3	
2	439	413	5	5	400	5	
3	212	198	11	3	167	13	
4	525	505	3	6	386	7	
5	158	152	15	3	136	17	
6	349	330	9	4	260	11	
7	307	297	17	4	280	15	
8	225	203	13	3	179	9	
9	438	414	1	5	399	1	
Out	3023	2872		38	2557		
10	370	360	4	5	350	4	
11	439	413	12	5	400	6	
12	212	198	10	4	167	14	
13	525	505	6	6	386	8	
14	158	152	16	3	136	18	
15	349	330	14	4	260	12	
16	307	297	18	4	280	16	
17	225	203	8	4	179	10	
18	438	414	2	5	399	2	
In	3023	2872		40	2557		
Total	6046	5744		78	5114		

cut along line

Woodland Greens GC — Fair Par Level 2

Hole	Blue	White	Hcp.	Par	Red	Hcp.	+/-
1	370	360	7	5	350	3	
2	439	413	5	6	400	5	
3	212	198	11	4	167	13	
4	525	505	3	7	386	7	
5	158	152	15	4	136	17	
6	349	330	9	5	260	11	
7	307	297	17	5	280	15	
8	225	203	13	4	179	9	
9	438	414	1	6	399	1	
Out	3023	2872		46	2557		
10	370	360	4	5	350	4	
11	439	413	12	6	400	6	
12	212	198	10	4	167	14	
13	525	505	6	7	386	8	
14	158	152	16	4	136	18	
15	349	330	14	5	260	12	
16	307	297	18	5	280	16	
17	225	203	8	4	179	10	
18	438	414	2	6	399	2	
In	3023	2872		46	2557		
Total	6046	5744		92	5114		

Agawam Hunt

Fair Par
Level 1

cut along line

For more information and
additional scorecards contact:
www.fairpar.com
or 401-782-0324

Agawam Hunt

Golfers and course operators are
encouraged to report changes in
course information to
Bogey Press
PO Box 5332
Wakefield RI 02880

Copyright © Stephen C. Heffner

Fair Par
Level 2

Agawam Hunt — Fair Par Level 1

Hole	Blue	White	Hcp.	Par	Red	Hcp.	+/-
1	422	400	3	5	393	4	
2	175	162	7	3	126	10	
3	502	475	5	6	467	2	
4	510	475	9	6	438	12	
5	168	145	15	3	131	18	
6	463	437	1	5	426	6	
7	293	266	13	4	256	14	
8	155	128	17	3	95	16	
9	347	329	11	4	326	8	
Out	3035	2817		39	2658		
10	388	383	8	5	380	7	
11	165	140	16	3	137	13	
12	412	407	6	5	406	17	
13	379	374	2	5	369	1	
14	355	346	12	4	341	11	
15	565	541	10	6	475	5	
16	175	162	14	3	151	9	
17	360	336	18	4	324	15	
18	439	410	4	5	396	3	
In	3238	3099		40	2886		
Total	6273	5916		79	5544		

— cut along line —

Agawam Hunt — Fair Par Level 2

Hole	Blue	White	Hcp.	Par	Red	Hcp.	+/-
1	422	400	3	6	393	4	
2	175	162	7	4	126	10	
3	502	475	5	6	467	2	
4	510	475	9	6	438	12	
5	168	145	15	4	131	18	
6	463	437	1	6	426	6	
7	293	266	13	5	256	14	
8	155	128	17	4	95	16	
9	347	329	11	5	326	8	
Out	3035	2817		46	2658		
10	388	383	8	5	380	7	
11	165	140	16	4	137	13	
12	412	407	6	6	406	17	
13	379	374	2	5	369	1	
14	355	346	12	5	341	11	
15	565	541	10	7	475	5	
16	175	162	14	4	151	9	
17	360	336	18	5	324	15	
18	439	410	4	6	396	3	
In	3238	3099		47	2886		
Total	6273	5916		93	5544		

For more information and
additional scorecards contact:
www.fairpar.com
or 401-782-0324

Golfers and course operators are
encouraged to report changes in
course information to
Bogey Press
PO Box 5332
Wakefield RI 02880

Alpine Country Club

Fair Par Level 1

--------- cut along line ---------

For more information and
additional scorecards contact:
www.fairpar.com
or 401-782-0324

Golfers and course operators are
encouraged to report changes in
course information to
Bogey Press
PO Box 5332
Wakefield RI 02880

Alpine Country Club

Fair Par Level 2

Fair Par Level 1

Hole	Blue	White	Hcp.	Par			Red	Hcp.	+/-
1	334	306	15	4			300	11	
2	521	510	5	6			410	7	
3	334	318	11	4			305	13	
4	513	503	7	6			480	5	
5	453	438	1	5			398	1	
6	226	205	13	3			180	15	
7	353	335	9	4			315	9	
8	553	540	3	6			445	3	
9	155	141	17	3			120	17	
Out	3442	3296		41			2953		
10	511	490	16	6			485	6	
11	371	361	8	4			348	10	
12	177	164	14	3			150	18	
13	412	395	2	5			375	2	
14	394	362	12	4			348	12	
15	173	155	18	3			138	16	
16	388	374	10	5			340	4	
17	409	390	6	5			350	14	
18	438	420	4	5			414	8	
In	3273	3111		40			2948		
Total	6715	6407		81			5901		

Alpine Country Club

— cut along line —

Fair Par Level 2

Hole	Blue	White	Hcp.	Par			Red	Hcp.	+/-
1	334	306	15	5			300	11	
2	521	510	5	7			410	7	
3	334	318	11	5			305	13	
4	513	503	7	7			480	5	
5	453	438	1	6			398	1	
6	226	205	13	4			180	15	
7	353	335	9	5			315	9	
8	553	540	3	7			445	3	
9	155	141	17	4			120	17	
Out	3442	3296		50			2953		
10	511	490	16	6			485	6	
11	371	361	8	5			348	10	
12	177	164	14	4			150	18	
13	412	395	2	5			375	2	
14	394	362	12	5			348	12	
15	173	155	18	4			138	16	
16	388	374	10	5			340	4	
17	409	390	6	5			350	14	
18	438	420	4	6			414	8	
In	3273	3111		45			2948		
Total	6715	6407		95			5901		

Alpine Country Club

Glocester Country Club

Fair Par Level 1

cut along line

Glocester Country Club

Fair Par Level 2

Glocester Country Club — Fair Par Level 1

Hole	Blue	White	Hcp. W/B	Par	Red/Gold	Hcp. R/G	+/-
1	335	325	5	5	317	5	
2	175	153	11	3	113	17	
3	485	477	15	6	468	1	
4	352	345	3	4	338	3	
5	411	401	1	5	390	7	
6	254	246	17	4	234	15	
7	322	297	7	4	282	13	
8	305	290	9	4	283	9	
9	163	158	13	3	116	11	
Out	2802	2692		38	2541		
10	335	325	8	5	317	6	
11	175	153	6	3	123	18	
12	485	477	16	6	468	2	
13	352	345	4	4	338	4	
14	411	401	2	5	390	8	
15	254	246	18	4	234	16	
16	322	297	10	4	282	14	
17	305	290	12	4	283	10	
18	163	158	14	3	129	12	
In	2802	2692		38	2564		
Total	5604	5384		76	5105		

— cut along line —

Glocester Country Club — Fair Par Level 2

Hole	Blue	White	Hcp. W/B	Par	Red/Gold	Hcp. R/G	+/-
1	335	325	5	5	317	5	
2	175	153	11	4	113	17	
3	485	477	15	6	468	1	
4	352	345	3	5	338	3	
5	411	401	1	6	390	7	
6	254	246	17	5	234	15	
7	322	297	7	5	282	13	
8	305	290	9	5	283	9	
9	163	158	13	4	116	11	
Out	2802	2692		45	2541		
10	335	325	8	5	317	6	
11	175	153	6	4	123	18	
12	485	477	16	6	468	2	
13	352	345	4	5	338	4	
14	411	401	2	6	390	8	
15	254	246	18	5	234	16	
16	322	297	10	5	282	14	
17	305	290	12	5	283	10	
18	163	158	14	4	129	12	
In	2802	2692		45	2564		
Total	5604	5384		90	5105		

Kirkbrae Country Club

Fair Par Level 1

For more information and additional scorecards contact:
www.fairpar.com
or 401-782-0324

Golfers and course operators are encouraged to report changes in course information to
Bogey Press
PO Box 5332
Wakefield RI 02880

---

cut along line

Kirbrae Country Club

Fair Par Level 2

For more information and additional scorecards contact:
www.fairpar.com
or 401-782-0324

Golfers and course operators are encouraged to report changes in course information to
Bogey Press
PO Box 5332
Wakefield RI 02880

Top scorecard:

Hole	Kirkbrae Country Club Gold	Blue	White	Hcp.	Par	Fair Par Level 1 Red	Hcp.	+/-
1	353	337	330	13	4	321	13	
2	387	369	357	7	5	349	11	
3	514	503	497	3	6	484	1	
4	141	129	129	17	3	107	15	
5	390	379	358	9	5	346	9	
6	456	445	429	5	5	421	5	
7	393	373	357	11	5	349	7	
8	444	424	412	1	5	399	3	
9	194	174	157	15	3	137	17	
Out	3272	3133	3026		41	2913		
10	324	306	285	6	4	274	14	
11	411	395	377	12	5	362	12	
12	479	474	470	4	5	463	4	
13	375	361	354	8	5	347	8	
14	502	494	440	2	6	425	2	
15	184	159	134	18	3	122	18	
16	326	306	300	14	4	287	10	
17	220	191	176	16	3	166	16	
18	456	445	392	10	5	402	6	
In	3277	3131	2928		40	2848		
Total	6549	6264	5954		81	5761		

cut along line

Bottom scorecard:

Hole	Kirkbrae Country Club Gold	Blue	White	Hcp.	Par	Fair Par Level 2 Red	Hcp.	+/-
1	353	337	330	13	5	321	13	
2	387	369	357	7	5	349	11	
3	514	503	497	3	7	484	1	
4	141	129	129	17	4	107	15	
5	390	379	358	9	5	346	9	
6	456	445	429	5	6	421	5	
7	393	373	357	11	5	349	7	
8	444	424	412	1	6	399	3	
9	194	174	157	15	4	137	17	
Out	3272	3133	3026		47	2913		
10	324	306	285	6	5	274	14	
11	411	395	377	12	5	362	12	
12	479	474	470	4	6	463	4	
13	375	361	354	8	5	347	8	
14	502	494	440	2	7	425	2	
15	184	159	134	18	4	122	18	
16	326	306	300	14	5	287	10	
17	220	191	176	16	4	166	16	
18	456	445	392	10	6	402	6	
In	3277	3131	2928		47	2848		
Total	6549	6264	5954		94	5761		

For more information and
additional scorecards contact:
www.fairpar.com
or 401-782-0324

Golfers and course operators are
encouraged to report changes in
course information to
Bogey Press
PO Box 5332
Wakefield RI 02880

Lincoln Country Club

Fair Par Level 1

---

cut along line

For more information and
additional scorecards contact:
www.fairpar.com
or 401-782-0324

Golfers and course operators are
encouraged to report changes in
course information to
Bogey Press
PO Box 5332
Wakefield RI 02880

Lincoln Country Club

Fair Par Level 2

Lincoln Country Club — Fair Par Level 1

Hole	Blue	White	Hcp.	Par	Red/Gold	Hcp.	+/-
1	381	346	4	5	295	10	
2	352	345	12	4	336	8	
3	154	138	16	3	125	14	
4	371	359	2	5	347	2	
5	335	314	14	4	284	12	
6	463	451	8	6	401	4	
7	327	311	10	4	226	16	
8	131	115	18	3	103	18	
9	398	372	6	5	332	6	
Out	2912	2751		39	2449		
10	381	346	3	5	333	9	
11	353	345	11	4	341	7	
12	154	138	15	3	130	13	
13	371	359	1	5	359	1	
14	335	314	13	4	306	11	
15	463	451	7	6	406	3	
16	327	311	9	4	234	15	
17	131	115	17	3	110	17	
18	398	372	5	5	401	5	
In	2912	2751		39	2620		
Total	5824	5502		78	5069		

---

cut along line

Lincoln Country Club — Fair Par Level 2

Hole	Blue	White	Hcp.	Par	Red/Gold	Hcp.	+/-
1	381	346	4	5	295	10	
2	352	345	12	5	336	8	
3	154	138	16	4	125	14	
4	371	359	2	5	347	2	
5	335	314	14	5	284	12	
6	463	451	8	7	401	4	
7	327	311	10	5	226	16	
8	131	115	18	4	103	18	
9	398	372	6	5	332	6	
Out	2912	2751		45	2449		
10	381	346	3	5	333	9	
11	353	345	11	5	341	7	
12	154	138	15	4	130	13	
13	371	359	1	5	359	1	
14	335	314	13	5	306	11	
15	463	451	7	7	406	3	
16	327	311	9	5	234	15	
17	131	115	17	4	110	17	
18	398	372	5	5	401	5	
In	2912	2751		45	2620		
Total	5824	5502		90	5069		

Louisquissett Golf Club

Fair Par
Level 1

─────── cut along line ───────

Louisquisset Golf Club

Fair Par
Level 2

Louisquisset Golf Club — Fair Par Level 1

Hole	Blue	White	Hcp. W/B	Par W/B	Red	Hcp.	+/-
1	385	371	2	5	312	4	
2	295	289	18	4	249	16	
3	450	440	10	6	285	8	
4	164	148	16	3	140	18	
5	187	172	12	3	155	12	
6	383	373	4	5	262	14	
7	328	318	8	4	240	6	
8	116	106	14	3	104	10	
9	375	351	6	5	316	2	
Out	2683	2568		38	2063		
10	385	371	1	5	312	3	
11	295	289	17	4	262	15	
12	450	440	9	6	388	7	
13	164	148	15	3	140	17	
14	187	172	11	4	155	13	
15	383	373	5	5	373	9	
16	328	318	7	4	240	5	
17	116	106	13	3	116	11	
18	375	351	3	5	316	1	
In	2683	2568		39	2302		
Total	5366	5136		77	4365		

----- cut along line -----

Louisquisset Golf Club — Fair Par Level 2

Hole	Blue	White	Hcp. W/B	Par W/B	Red	Hcp.	+/-
1	385	371	2	6	312	4	
2	295	289	18	5	249	16	
3	450	440	10	6	285	8	
4	164	148	16	4	140	18	
5	187	172	12	4	155	12	
6	383	373	4	6	262	14	
7	328	318	8	5	240	6	
8	116	106	14	4	104	10	
9	375	351	6	6	316	2	
Out	2683	2568		46	2063		
10	385	371	1	6	312	3	
11	295	289	17	5	262	15	
12	450	440	9	6	388	7	
13	164	148	15	4	140	17	
14	187	172	11	4	155	13	
15	383	373	5	6	373	9	
16	328	318	7	5	240	5	
17	116	106	13	4	116	11	
18	375	351	3	6	316	1	
In	2683	2568		46	2302		
Total	5366	5136		92	4365		

For more information and
additional scorecards contact:
www.fairpar.com
or 401-782-0324

Golfers and course operators are
encouraged to report changes in
course information to
Bogey Press
PO Box 5332
Wakefield RI 02880

Metacomet
Country
Club

Fair Par
Level 1

cut along line

For more information and
additional scorecards contact:
www.fairpar.com
or 401-782-0324

Golfers and course operators are
encouraged to report changes in
course information to
Bogey Press
PO Box 5332
Wakefield RI 02880

Metacomet
Country
Club

Fair Par
Level 2

Metacomet Country Club — Fair Par Level 1

Hole	Blue	White Hcp.	Par	Red	Hcp.	+/-
1	386	11	5	367	9	
2	472	7	5	428	3	
3	359	5	5	350	11	
4	446	1	5	370	7	
5	180	15	3	150	15	
6	441	3	5	400	5	
7	160	17	3	139	17	
8	358	13	4	340	13	
9	463	9	5	449	1	
Out	3265		40	2993		
10	228	16	4	182	16	
11	378	10	4	359	6	
12	242	18	4	135	18	
13	423	6	5	325	14	
14	448	2	5	435	2	
15	384	8	5	352	8	
16	347	12	4	339	10	
17	402	4	5	390	4	
18	347	14	4	335	12	
In	3199		40	2852		
Total	6464		80	5845		

cut along line

Metacomet Country Club — Fair Par Level 2

Hole	Blue	White Hcp.	Par	Red	Hcp.	+/-
1	386	11	6	367	9	
2	472	7	6	428	3	
3	359	5	5	350	11	
4	446	1	6	370	7	
5	180	15	4	150	15	
6	441	3	6	400	5	
7	160	17	4	139	17	
8	358	13	5	340	13	
9	463	9	6	449	1	
Out	3265		48	2993		
10	228	16	4	182	16	
11	378	10	5	359	6	
12	242	18	4	135	18	
13	423	6	6	325	14	
14	448	2	6	435	2	
15	384	8	6	352	8	
16	347	12	5	339	10	
17	402	4	6	390	4	
18	347	14	5	335	12	
In	3199		47	2852		
Total	6464		95	5845		

The Misquamicut Club

Fair Par Level 1

cut along line

The Misquamicut Club

Fair Par Level 2

Misquamicut Club — Par — Fair Par Level 1

Hole	Blue	White	Hcp.	Par	Red	Hcp.	+/-
1	382	379	7	5	376	7	
2	433	395	1	5	391	1	
3	230	221	13	4	198	13	
4	272	257	11	4	249	11	
5	424	388	5	5	382	5	
6	194	185	15	4	143	17	
7	522	472	3	6	468	3	
8	165	155	17	3	149	15	
9	359	353	9	5	258	9	
Out	2981	2805		41	2614		
10	381	366	12	5	358	4	
11	323	308	16	4	294	14	
12	169	127	18	3	119	16	
13	431	403	4	5	363	2	
14	435	427	2	5	422	8	
15	363	351	10	4	344	6	
16	391	342	8	4	338	12	
17	525	440	6	6	410	10	
18	215	191	14	4	133	18	
In	3233	2955		40	2781		
Total	6214	5760		81	5395		

--- cut along line ---

Misquamicut Club — Par — Fair Par Level 2

Hole	Blue	White	Hcp.	Par	Red	Hcp.	+/-
1	382	379	7	6	376	7	
2	433	395	1	6	391	1	
3	230	221	13	4	198	13	
4	272	257	11	5	249	11	
5	424	388	5	5	382	5	
6	194	185	15	4	143	17	
7	522	472	3	6	468	3	
8	165	155	17	4	149	15	
9	359	353	9	5	258	9	
Out	2981	2805		45	2614		
10	381	366	12	5	358	4	
11	323	308	16	5	294	14	
12	169	127	18	4	119	16	
13	431	403	4	6	363	2	
14	435	427	2	6	422	8	
15	363	351	10	5	344	6	
16	391	342	8	5	338	12	
17	525	440	6	6	410	10	
18	215	191	14	4	133	18	
In	3233	2955		46	2781		
Total	6214	5760		91	5395		

Newport Country Club

Fair Par Level 1

cut along line

Newport Country Club

Fair Par Level 2

Newport Country Club — Fair Par Level 1

Hole	Red	White	Hcp.		Par		Blue	Hcp.	+/-
1	481	442	15		6		427	9	
2	366	352	9		5		341	5	
3	312	276	13		4		228	15	
4	211	181	7		3		181	11	
5	422	411	1		5		347	1	
6	356	304	11		4		283	13	
7	518	493	5		6		454	7	
8	177	164	17		3		155	17	
9	422	406	3		5		381	3	
Out	3265	3029			41		2797		
10	528	517	10		6		477	8	
11	298	289	18		4		245	18	
12	477	463	14		6		396	10	
13	151	137	16		3		123	16	
14	205	200	6		4		161	14	
15	399	391	2		5		386	2	
16	359	321	8		4		311	6	
17	428	397	4		5		380	4	
18	377	367	12		5		298	12	
In	3222	3082			42		2777		
Total	6487	6111			83		5574		

cut along line

Newport Country Club — Fair Par Level 2

Hole	Red	White	Hcp.		Par		Blue	Hcp.	+/-
1	481	442	15		6		427	9	
2	366	352	9		5		341	5	
3	312	276	13		5		228	15	
4	211	181	7		4		181	11	
5	422	411	1		6		347	1	
6	356	304	11		5		283	13	
7	518	493	5		7		454	7	
8	177	164	17		4		155	17	
9	422	406	3		6		381	3	
Out	3265	3029			48		2797		
10	528	517	10		7		477	8	
11	298	289	18		5		245	18	
12	477	463	14		6		396	10	
13	151	137	16		4		123	16	
14	205	200	6		4		161	14	
15	399	391	2		6		386	2	
16	359	321	8		5		311	6	
17	428	397	4		6		380	4	
18	377	367	12		5		298	12	
In	3222	3082			48		2777		
Total	6487	6111			96		5574		

For more information and
additional scorecards contact:
www.fairpar.com
or 401-782-0324

Golfers and course operators are
encouraged to report changes in
course information to
Bogey Press
PO Box 5332
Wakefield RI 02880

Pawtucket Country Club

Fair Par Level 1

cut along line

For more information and
additional scorecards contact:
www.fairpar.com
or 401-782-0324

Golfers and course operators are
encouraged to report changes in
course information to
Bogey Press
PO Box 5332
Wakefield RI 02880

Pawtucket Country Club

Fair Par Level 2

Pawtucket Country Club — Fair Par Level 1

Hole	Blue	White	Gold	Hcp.		Par		Red	Hcp.	+/-
1	389	380	375	9		5		370	9	
2	416	407	397	3		5		392	5	
3	379	369	340	11		5		330	13	
4	380	369	360	13		4		354	11	
5	188	173	165	15		3		156	15	
6	414	392	388	5		5		385	7	
7	173	161	150	17		3		143	17	
8	542	530	515	7		6		429	3	
9	449	436	430	1		5		425	1	
Out	3330	3217	3120			41		2984		
10	435	417	405	6		5		379	8	
11	308	296	285	14		4		280	14	
12	451	433	420	2		5		415	2	
13	186	176	170	16		3		167	16	
14	375	362	354	10		4		349	12	
15	170	154	140	18		3		130	18	
16	432	417	408	4		5		403	4	
17	434	410	402	8		5		397	6	
18	379	365	351	12		4		346	10	
In	3170	3030	2935			38		2866		
Total	6500	6247	6055			79		5850		

--- cut along line ---

Pawtucket Country Club — Fair Par Level 2

Hole	Blue	White	Gold	Hcp.		Par		Red	Hcp.	+/-
1	389	380	375	9		6		370	9	
2	416	407	397	3		6		392	5	
3	379	369	340	11		5		330	13	
4	380	369	360	13		5		354	11	
5	188	173	165	15		4		156	15	
6	414	392	388	5		6		385	7	
7	173	161	150	17		4		143	17	
8	542	530	515	7		7		429	3	
9	449	436	430	1		6		425	1	
Out	3330	3217	3120			49		2984		
10	435	417	405	6		6		379	8	
11	308	296	285	14		5		280	14	
12	451	433	420	2		6		415	2	
13	186	176	170	16		4		167	16	
14	375	362	354	10		5		349	12	
15	170	154	140	18		4		130	18	
16	432	417	408	4		6		403	4	
17	434	410	402	8		6		397	6	
18	379	365	351	12		5		346	10	
In	3170	3030	2935			47		2866		
Total	6500	6247	6055			96		5850		

Pt. Judith Country Club

Fair Par Level 1

cut along line

Pt. Judith Country Club

Fair Par Level 2

Pt. Judith Country Club — Fair Par Level 1

Hole	Blue	White	Gold	Hcp.	Par	Red	Hcp.	+/-
1	406	388	382	9	5	373	1	
2	365	350	326	5	4	317	9	
3	527	504	486	3	6	449	13	
4	316	291	234	17	4	228	17	
5	418	391	384	7	5	350	7	
6	354	347	343	11	4	338	5	
7	406	380	375	13	5	354	11	
8	425	403	381	1	5	357	3	
9	130	120	115	15	3	107	15	
Out	3347	3169	3026		41	2873		
10	454	402	382	2	5	377	2	
11	213	204	193	16	3	172	14	
12	324	313	300	18	4	289	16	
13	404	385	375	6	5	331	6	
14	338	326	306	12	4	293	4	
15	373	357	346	10	5	330	12	
16	217	196	154	14	3	151	10	
17	440	425	400	4	5	391	18	
18	594	567	536	8	6	454	8	
In	3357	3175	2992		40	2788		
Total	6704	6344	6018		81	5661		

- - - cut along line - - -

Pt. Judith Country Club — Fair Par Level 2

Hole	Blue	White	Gold	Hcp.	Par	Red	Hcp.	+/-
1	406	388	382	9	5	373	1	
2	365	350	326	5	5	317	9	
3	527	504	486	3	7	449	13	
4	316	291	234	17	5	228	17	
5	418	391	384	7	5	350	7	
6	354	347	343	11	5	338	5	
7	406	380	375	13	5	354	11	
8	425	403	381	1	6	357	3	
9	130	120	115	15	4	107	15	
Out	3347	3169	3026		47	2873		
10	454	402	382	2	6	377	2	
11	213	204	193	16	4	172	14	
12	324	313	300	18	5	289	16	
13	404	385	375	6	5	331	6	
14	338	326	306	12	5	293	4	
15	373	357	346	10	5	330	12	
16	217	196	154	14	4	151	10	
17	440	425	400	4	6	391	18	
18	594	567	536	8	7	454	8	
In	3357	3175	2992		47	2788		
Total	6704	6344	6018		94	5661		

Potowomut Golf Club

Fair Par
Level 1

— cut along line —

Potowomut Golf Club

Fair Par
Level 2

Fair Par Level 1 / Potowomut Golf Club

Hole	Blue	White	Hcp.	Par	Red	Hcp.	+/-
1	429	402	3	5	401	7	
2	362	342	9	5	336	1	
3	163	143	17	3	140	15	
4	370	352	15	5	329	13	
5	429	409	1	5	407	9	
6	199	179	11	3	176	17	
7	352	332	13	4	318	11	
8	406	386	7	5	370	3	
9	445	425	5	5	406	5	
Out	3155	2970		40	2883		
10	497	477	6	6	422	8	
11	355	335	16	4	333	10	
12	207	187	12	3	185	16	
13	323	313	14	4	282	12	
14	379	354	10	5	329	14	
15	527	507	2	6	412	2	
16	159	139	18	3	118	18	
17	391	371	8	5	367	4	
18	387	367	4	5	318	6	
In	3225	3050		41	2666		
Total	6380	6020		81	5649		

cut along line

Fair Par Level 2 / Potowomut Golf Club

Hole	Blue	White	Hcp.	Par	Red	Hcp.	+/-
1	429	402	3	6	401	7	
2	362	342	9	5	336	1	
3	163	143	17	4	140	15	
4	370	352	15	5	329	13	
5	429	409	1	6	407	9	
6	199	179	11	4	176	17	
7	352	332	13	5	318	11	
8	406	386	7	5	370	3	
9	445	425	5	6	406	5	
Out	3155	2970		46	2883		
10	497	477	6	6	422	8	
11	355	335	16	5	333	10	
12	207	187	12	4	185	16	
13	323	313	14	5	282	12	
14	379	354	10	5	329	14	
15	527	507	2	7	412	2	
16	159	139	18	4	118	18	
17	391	371	8	5	367	4	
18	387	367	4	6	318	6	
In	3225	3050		47	2666		
Total	6380	6020		93	5649		

For more information and
additional scorecards contact:
www.fairpar.com
or 401-782-0324

Golfers and course operators are
encouraged to report changes in
course information to
Bogey Press
PO Box 5332
Wakefield RI 02880

Quidnessett Country Club

Fair Par Level 1

— cut along line —

For more information and
additional scorecards contact:
www.fairpar.com
or 401-782-0324

Golfers and course operators are
encouraged to report changes in
course information to
Bogey Press
PO Box 5332
Wakefield RI 02880

Quidnessett Country Club

Fair Par Level 2

Quidnessett Country Club — Fair Par Level 1

Hole	Blue	White	Hcp.	Par	Red	Hcp.	+/-
1	379	365	9	5	349	9	
2	176	160	15	3	152	15	
3	548	505	11	6	497	1	
4	465	450	1	5	364	3	
5	214	168	13	3	125	17	
6	405	386	5	5	379	7	
7	422	413	3	5	375	5	
8	416	400	7	5	335	13	
9	516	496	17	6	480	11	
Out	3541	3343		43	3056		
10	412	392	2	5	372	2	
11	592	524	4	6	440	10	
12	185	169	16	3	130	18	
13	362	342	12	4	322	12	
14	526	506	10	6	420	8	
15	331	311	18	4	292	14	
16	181	166	14	3	109	16	
17	410	380	8	5	340	6	
18	400	367	6	5	355	4	
In	3399	3157		41	2780		
Total	6940	6500		84	5836		

— cut along line —

Quidnessett Country Club — Fair Par Level 2

Hole	Blue	White	Hcp.	Par	Red	Hcp.	+/-
1	379	365	9	5	349	9	
2	176	160	15	4	152	15	
3	548	505	11	7	497	1	
4	465	450	1	6	364	3	
5	214	168	13	4	125	17	
6	405	386	5	5	379	7	
7	422	413	3	6	375	5	
8	416	400	7	6	335	13	
9	516	496	17	6	480	11	
Out	3541	3343		49	3056		
10	412	392	2	6	372	2	
11	592	524	4	7	440	10	
12	185	169	16	4	130	18	
13	362	342	12	5	322	12	
14	526	506	10	7	420	8	
15	331	311	18	5	292	14	
16	181	166	14	4	109	16	
17	410	380	8	5	340	6	
18	400	367	6	5	355	4	
In	3399	3157		48	2780		
Total	6940	6500		97	5836		

For more information and
additional scorecards contact:
www.fairpar.com
or 401-782-0324

Golfers and course operators are
encouraged to report changes in
course information to
Bogey Press
PO Box 5332
Wakefield RI 02880

Rhode Island CC

Fair Par Level 1

cut along line

For more information and
additional scorecards contact:
www.fairpar.com
or 401-782-0324

Golfers and course operators are
encouraged to report changes in
course information to
Bogey Press
PO Box 5332
Wakefield RI 02880

Rhode Island CC

Fair Par Level 2

Rhode Island Country Club — Fair Par Level 1

Hole	Blue	White	Hcp.	Par	Red	Gold	Hcp.
1	411	359	15	5	359	357	11
2	374	366	5	5	366	298	5
3	344	311	7	4	265	261	13
4	356	347	11	4	347	272	7
5	144	144	17	3	144	127	17
6	295	264	9	4	264	260	9
7	451	430	1	5	430	360	3
8	480	438	13	6	438	356	1
9	422	414	3	5	414	362	15
Out	3227	3073		41	3027	2753	
10	195	178	16	4	178	170	16
11	511	501	6	6	427	422	4
12	306	292	14	4	292	198	10
13	440	426	2	5	426	423	14
14	376	362	4	5	362	359	2
15	361	316	10	4	316	311	12
16	385	373	12	5	373	371	6
17	133	120	18	3	120	116	18
18	388	332	8	5	332	268	8
In	3095	2900		41	2826	2638	
Total	6322	5973		82	5853	5391	

cut along line

Rhode Island Country Club — Fair Par Level 2

Hole	Blue	White	Hcp.	Par	Red	Gold	Hcp.
1	411	359	15	5	359	357	11
2	374	366	5	5	366	298	5
3	344	311	7	5	265	261	13
4	356	347	11	5	347	272	7
5	144	144	17	4	144	127	17
6	295	264	9	5	264	260	9
7	451	430	1	6	430	360	3
8	480	438	13	7	438	356	1
9	422	414	3	6	414	362	15
Out	3227	3073		48	3027	2753	
10	195	178	16	4	178	170	16
11	511	501	6	7	427	422	4
12	306	292	14	5	292	198	10
13	440	426	2	6	426	423	14
14	376	362	4	6	362	359	2
15	361	316	10	5	316	311	12
16	385	373	12	6	373	371	6
17	133	120	18	4	120	116	18
18	388	332	8	6	332	268	8
In	3095	2900		49	2826	2638	
Total	6322	5973		97	5853	5391	

Sakonnet Golf Club

Fair Par Level 1

For more information and
additional scorecards contact:
www.fairpar.com
or 401-782-0324

Golfers and course operators are
encouraged to report changes in
course information to
Bogey Press
PO Box 5332
Wakefield RI 02880

--- cut along line ---

Sakonnet Golf Club

Fair Par Level 2

For more information and
additional scorecards contact:
www.fairpar.com
or 401-782-0324

Golfers and course operators are
encouraged to report changes in
course information to
Bogey Press
PO Box 5332
Wakefield RI 02880

Sakonnet Golf Club — Fair Par Level 1

Hole	Blue	Hcp.		Par		White	Hcp.	+/-
1	377	5		5		369	9	
2	180	17		3		155	17	
3	477	11		6		469	1	
4	404	1		5		392	5	
5	364	15		4		353	13	
6	213	13		4		160	15	
7	360	7		4		351	3	
8	342	9		4		320	7	
9	393	3		5		331	11	
Out	3110			40		2900		
10	159	18		3		143	18	
11	480	10		6		425	4	
12	414	2		5		392	14	
13	318	6		4		304	6	
14	187	14		3		175	8	
15	407	4		5		390	2	
16	156	16		3		138	16	
17	320	12		4		294	12	
18	340	8		4		286	10	
In	2781			37		2547		
Total	5891			77		5447		

cut along line

Sakonnet Golf Club — Fair Par Level 2

Hole	Blue	Hcp.		Par		White	Hcp.	+/-
1	377	5		5		369	9	
2	180	17		4		155	17	
3	477	11		7		469	1	
4	404	1		6		392	5	
5	364	15		5		353	13	
6	213	13		4		160	15	
7	360	7		5		351	3	
8	342	9		5		320	7	
9	393	3		6		331	11	
Out	3110			47		2900		
10	159	18		4		143	18	
11	480	10		6		425	4	
12	414	2		6		392	14	
13	318	6		5		304	6	
14	187	14		4		175	8	
15	407	4		6		390	2	
16	156	16		4		138	16	
17	320	12		5		294	12	
18	340	8		5		286	10	
In	2781			45		2547		
Total	5891			92		5447		

For more information and
additional scorecards contact:
www.fairpar.com
or 401-782-0324

Golfers and course operators are
encouraged to report changes in
course information to
Bogey Press
PO Box 5332
Wakefield RI 02880

Valley Country Club

Fair Par Level 1

---

cut along line

For more information and
additional scorecards contact:
www.fairpar.com
or 401-782-0324

Golfers and course operators are
encouraged to report changes in
course information to
Bogey Press
PO Box 5332
Wakefield RI 02880

Valley Country Club

Fair Par Level 2

Valley Country Club — Fair Par Level 1

Hole	Blue	White	Hcp.	Par	Red	Hcp.	+/-
1	360	354	9	5	333	11	
2	603	569	1	6	531	1	
3	362	315	17	4	281	13	
4	383	367	7	5	349	7	
5	502	491	11	6	478	3	
6	159	146	15	3	139	15	
7	381	368	5	4	362	5	
8	215	200	13	3	176	17	
9	397	383	3	5	361	9	
Out	3362	3193		41	3010		
10	389	372	8	5	345	8	
11	367	352	4	5	288	12	
12	207	188	2	4	99	18	
13	395	385	14	5	365	6	
14	364	341	16	4	313	14	
15	339	328	6	4	315	4	
16	470	456	18	5	442	2	
17	182	162	10	3	137	16	
18	548	516	12	6	434	10	
In	3261	3100		41	2738		
Total	6623	6293		82	5748		

— cut along line —

Valley Country Club — Fair Par Level 2

Hole	Blue	White	Hcp.	Par	Red	Hcp.	+/-
1	360	354	9	5	333	11	
2	603	569	1	7	531	1	
3	362	315	17	5	281	13	
4	383	367	7	5	349	7	
5	502	491	11	7	478	3	
6	159	146	15	4	139	15	
7	381	368	5	5	362	5	
8	215	200	13	4	176	17	
9	397	383	3	5	361	9	
Out	3362	3193		47	3010		
10	389	372	8	5	345	8	
11	367	352	4	6	288	12	
12	207	188	2	4	99	18	
13	395	385	14	5	365	6	
14	364	341	16	5	313	14	
15	339	328	6	5	315	4	
16	470	456	18	6	442	2	
17	182	162	10	4	137	16	
18	548	516	12	7	434	10	
In	3261	3100		47	2738		
Total	6623	6293		94	5748		

Wannamoisett Country Club

Fair Par Level 1

---

cut along line

Wannamoisett Country Club

Fair Par Level 2

Wannamoisett Country Club — Fair Par Level 1

Hole	Blue	White	Hcp.	Par	Red	Hcp.	+/-
1	428	420	9	5	411	13	
2	474	456	3	5	410	11	
3	138	127	17	3	105	17	
4	445	440	1	5	350	9	
5	379	364	11	5	339	5	
6	429	415	7	5	389	1	
7	347	335	13	4	325	7	
8	183	175	15	3	167	15	
9	443	428	5	5	402	3	
Out	3266	3160		40	2898		
10	416	399	6	5	377	10	
11	393	386	10	5	368	2	
12	215	200	16	4	178	12	
13	383	361	14	4	341	8	
14	368	353	8	4	345	6	
15	200	187	18	3	176	16	
16	429	404	2	5	390	14	
17	545	533	12	6	495	4	
18	446	416	4	5	376	18	
In	3395	3239		41	3046		
Total	6661	6399		81	5944		

— cut along line —

Wannamoisett Country Club — Fair Par Level 2

Hole	Blue	White	Hcp.	Par	Red	Hcp.	+/-
1	428	420	9	6	411	13	
2	474	456	3	6	410	11	
3	138	127	17	4	105	17	
4	445	440	1	6	350	9	
5	379	364	11	5	339	5	
6	429	415	7	6	389	1	
7	347	335	13	5	325	7	
8	183	175	15	4	167	15	
9	443	428	5	6	402	3	
Out	3266	3160		48	2898		
10	416	399	6	6	377	10	
11	393	386	10	5	368	2	
12	215	200	16	4	178	12	
13	383	361	14	5	341	8	
14	368	353	8	5	345	6	
15	200	187	18	4	176	16	
16	429	404	2	6	390	14	
17	545	533	12	7	495	4	
18	446	416	4	6	376	18	
In	3395	3239		48	3046		
Total	6661	6399		96	5944		

Wanumetonomy Golf & CC

Fair Par Level 1

cut along line

Wanumetonomy Golf & CC

Fair Par Level 2

Wanumetonomy Golf & Country Club — Fair Par Level 1

Hole	Blue	White	Hcp.	Par		Red	Hcp.	+/-
1		313	13	4		293	13	
2		311	11	4		290	15	
3		453	1	5		420	5	
4		377	7	5		368	1	
5		151	15	3		131	17	
6		405	3	5		385	7	
7		292	17	4		290	11	
8		370	5	5		333	3	
9		338	9	4		291	9	
Out		3010		39		2801		
10		392	4	5		327	4	
11		400	10	5		396	8	
12		175	18	3		160	16	
13		342	14	5		327	14	
14		333	16	4		322	12	
15		399	2	5		377	10	
16		556	6	6		441	6	
17		201	12	3		154	18	
18		380	8	5		342	2	
In		3178		41		2846		
Total		6188		80		5647		

— cut along line —

Wanumetonomy Golf & Country Club — Fair Par Level 2

Hole	Blue	White	Hcp.	Par		Red	Hcp.	+/-
1		313	13	5		293	13	
2		311	11	5		290	15	
3		453	1	6		420	5	
4		377	7	5		368	1	
5		151	15	4		131	17	
6		405	3	6		385	7	
7		292	17	5		290	11	
8		370	5	5		333	3	
9		338	9	5		291	9	
Out		3010		46		2801		
10		392	4	6		327	4	
11		400	10	5		396	8	
12		175	18	4		160	16	
13		342	14	5		327	14	
14		333	16	5		322	12	
15		399	2	6		377	10	
16		556	6	7		441	6	
17		201	12	4		154	18	
18		380	8	5		342	2	
In		3178		47		2846		
Total		6188		93		5647		

For more information and
additional scorecards contact:
www.fairpar.com
or 401-782-0324

Golfers and course operators are
encouraged to report changes in
course information to
Bogey Press
PO Box 5332
Wakefield RI 02880

Warwick Country Club

Fair Par Level 1

— cut along line —

For more information and
additional scorecards contact:
www.fairpar.com
or 401-782-0324

Golfers and course operators are
encouraged to report changes in
course information to
Bogey Press
PO Box 5332
Wakefield RI 02880

Warwick Country Club

Fair Par Level 2

Warwick Country Club — Fair Par Level 1

Hole	Blue	White	Hcp.	Par	Red	Hcp.	+/-
1	451	439	1	5	432	3	
2	363	354	11	4	346	13	
3	382	373	5	5	356	5	
4	399	388	9	5	379	7	
5	418	406	3	5	353	1	
6	338	331	17	4	317	9	
7	197	182	13	3	135	17	
8	393	378	7	5	364	11	
9	184	165	15	3	110	15	
Out	3125	3016		39	2792		
10	438	431	4	5	337	8	
11	379	368	10	5	349	12	
12	412	406	6	5	400	10	
13	186	178	18	3	152	16	
14	355	332	12	4	315	14	
15	478	472	14	6	452	2	
16	460	451	2	5	434	4	
17	212	198	16	3	175	18	
18	422	417	8	5	409	6	
In	3342	3253		41	3023		
Total	6467	6269		80	5815		

—————————————— cut along line ——————————————

Warwick Country Club — Fair Par Level 2

Hole	Blue	White	Hcp.	Par	Red	Hcp.	+/-
1	451	439	1	6	432	3	
2	363	354	11	5	346	13	
3	382	373	5	5	356	5	
4	399	388	9	5	379	7	
5	418	406	3	6	353	1	
6	338	331	17	5	317	9	
7	197	182	13	4	135	17	
8	393	378	7	5	364	11	
9	184	165	15	4	110	15	
Out	3125	3016		45	2792		
10	438	431	4	6	337	8	
11	379	368	10	5	349	12	
12	412	406	6	6	400	10	
13	186	178	18	4	152	16	
14	355	332	12	5	315	14	
15	478	472	14	6	452	2	
16	460	451	2	6	434	4	
17	212	198	16	4	175	18	
18	422	417	8	6	409	6	
In	3342	3253		48	3023		
Total	6467	6269		93	5815		